STUCK IN THE PASSING LANE

A MEMOIR

STUCK IN THE PASSING LANE

A MEMOIR

JED RINGEL

ABOUTFACE
PRESS

Copyright © by 2015 Jed S. Ringel

Published by About Face Press LLC, Montauk, NY

ABOUT FACE
PRESS
www.aboutfacepress.com

Paperback ISBN: 978-0-9862550-0-7
eBook ISBN: 978-0-9862550-1-4

Cover and Interior Design by GKS Creative

Printed in the United States of America

All rights reserved. No part of this publication may be reproduced or transmitted in any form or by any means, electronic or mechanical, including photocopying, recording, or any other information storage and retrieval system, without the written permission of the publisher.

This book is based on real events occurring around the time of my divorce. However, names and identifying characteristics have been changed. The book, though, remains an accurate depiction of my experience.

Publisher's Cataloging-In-Publication Data
(Prepared by The Donohue Group, Inc.)

Ringel, Jed.
  Stuck in the passing lane : a memoir / Jed Ringel.

  pages ; cm

  Issued also as an ebook.
  ISBN: 978-0-9862550-0-7 (paperback)

  1. Ringel, Jed. 2. Divorced men--Biography. 3. Dating (Social customs) 4. Man-woman relationships. 5. Divorced men--Conduct of life. I. Title.

HQ811.5.R56 A3 2015
306.89/2092

*For my grandfather, Samuel Glasberg,
who taught me how to skip*

Contents

Baby Boomer Blues	1
Unnatural Selection	23
I Can't Take Me Anywhere	37
Miss-Stepping Stones	47
I Wish I Had a Picture . . .	73
Houston, We Have a Problem	87
Stuck in the Passing Lane	123
Behind the Iron Curtain's Green Door	139
Life Expectancies	171
Unintelligent Design	191
Life's a Beach	211
The Heart is a Lonely Punter	219
Missing in Beijing	245
A Second Coming	269
Epilogue	277

BABY BOOMER BLUES

I'm lounging beside an abandoned swimming pool surrounded by chicken coops, barns and servants' quarters, remnants of an eighteenth-century dairy farm. The old farmhouse is the only rental I could find near what's been my family's home for the past fifteen years. I moved out of that place, and I'm waiting (and waiting) for my STBE's (soon-to-be-ex's) agreement to a house-switching plan allowing my three daughters to stay with me on alternate weeks.

I'm reading *Atonement* on a lounge chair badly needing re-webbing. Well, not exactly *reading*. I'm thinking about the time of day, but not in human time. I'm trying to imagine time in a way that my dog, Kobi, lying in the Aboriginal-looking stone hut in the corner, might see it. Broad periods. *Dinnertime! Where's-my-fucking-dinner-already time!*

The sun's passing overhead, qualifying this as late afternoon, which means time for the second bottle of wine

I'm reaching for under the bird-shit-covered chaise. I'm about to consume it now that it's *late* afternoon, a time safely distant from the first bottle finished in the *early* afternoon, an hour ago. My cell phone rings. Damn, it's hard uncorking and answering.

She says she liked my message. *What message?* I think, cursing myself.

"You liked the uh . . ."

"You don't know who I am? That's okay," she says. "Fulbright scholar? Op-ed page of the *Times*? Ring a bell? Good looks. Writes books."

"Yeah," I exclaim, excited, I guess, by actually remembering a personal ad I responded to a couple of weeks ago from the classifieds of *The New York Review of Books*. It was, I thought, an absurd foray because, really, how many sexy dream women do you think advertise in droning intellectual magazines?

"You're enthusiastic," she says.

"No," I say, hoping I don't sound desperate. "I mean there's a lot of noise here." I hold the phone out so she hears the lawn mowers next door. "Sure, I remember," I continue, and I did, particularly the twenty-five buck bill for calling the phone number the magazine assigned her for hearing from guys like me.

"You've got a great act, but you're pushing it."

"Act?"

"I'm kidding. You really haven't done this before?"

"Not really," I say, which is true about personals,

though I know she's talking about the entire arsenal of dating weaponry created during my twenty-three-year marriage-induced dating siesta. "Are you, uh, divorced?" I ask.

"Little over three years. We're still friends. He's back in Argentina. His first wife made him so miserable. Wouldn't let him see his kids. He finally went back to her."

"And do you have . . ."

"Wonderful guy. Professional tennis player."

"So you're, uh . . ." I stop because I have no idea what to ask, my focus having shifted from this seemingly yielding woman to my unyielding cork.

"Are you reading anything?" she asks, relieving me from this increasingly awkward pause, during which I improve my grip enough to yank hard, striking wine.

"No," I say. But then I realize that she doesn't mean *right now*, as in while we're talking. "Actually, I'm working my way through *Atonement*," I add, hoping the change in answer doesn't sound like I'm making things up.

"Much better than his new book, *Saturday Night*. But McEwan's writing's so workmanlike, so studied, don't you think? You're not a conservative, are you?"

"I grew up during the Vietnam War."

"I've been reading the Clark book on Iraq," she says. "That should be the end of it, even for conservatives. 'We don't nation-build.' 'We don't use the military unless absolutely necessary.'"

"What did you do on the Fulbright?"

"I can't seem to find people who read anymore," she says. "*The Da Vinci Code* and all that crap."

She wasn't answering the Fulbright question, but she wasn't evasive either. Or rating me. She was just on her own trip, in her own world. Fulbright *shmulbright*. Some world-renowned intellectual thing. Argentinean tennis player? Don't they all look like Antonio Banderas? So she's Salma Hayek? Penelope Cruz? Gorgeous, ditzy, smart, sweet. That'd be different.

I'm startled by the warm breath on my ear.

"Who's that?" an almondy, clean-scrubbed smelling voice whispers.

Cara intruding in my life unannounced, *again*. Her lips trace my neck. I panic.

"Can I put you on hold for a second?" I say to the woman whose name I've either forgotten or not been told, hoping I'm hitting the hold button, though I can't see the little letters without my glasses, which will take much too long to find.

"My cousin," I whisper to Cara, who, backing off from my neck, makes room for me to face her. Little white teeth, the ones that sometimes inadvertently grate me, give a piranha-like look to her otherwise childish face. Her straight, black, glistening Mayan hair reflects the sun. Her mulatto skin is as smooth and tan as the fresh empanadas in the take-out tin she's passing under my nose.

"Give me a minute?" I whisper, not really caring what Cara suspects. After all, she tolerates me not returning her calls, being drunk, leaving her house the instant I want, pretty much telling her when to leave mine, usually soon after sex. Cara straightens up and moves back a bit. I implore with my eyes. She sighs and shrugs, feigning exasperation. I imagine she learned this expression from her mother and grandmother, matronly Puerto Rican women who probably gave the same response to their Zorro-lookalike philandering husbands, men aging like good steak, as they headed out for nights with *amigos* and *señoritas*, knowing that all they really had to do to keep their wives in tow was to come home.

"My cousin. The one in Florida. The one who's ill," I mouth to Cara, creasing my eyes for sympathy, not wanting to push my luck with this girl who's so easy, her white blouse sheer in the sunlight as she turns, already no bra, probably naked under her formal blue work dress. She heads to the old farmhouse, turning back briefly to make sure that I'm watching.

"Would you like to meet in the city?" I ask the caller.

"No phone romances for you," she says.

I'm not sure what that means, but I'm glad she's not asking why I'm rushing.

"You like French?" she continues.

"*Bien sûr*," I say, wondering why I'm egging on someone I want to move along.

"Know *Bistro Français Les Routiers*?"

"I, uh . . ."

"Amsterdam Avenue. I'll make a reservation for seven Friday."

"Tomorrow?"

"Yeah. I'm in the Apthorp. 78th and Broadway. See you."

"Wait! . . . Who do I ask for?"

"Rene Flanello."

I make it out of the pool enclosure, surprised that I remember to close the gate. Though Cara is waiting, I'm taking my time. Opening the screen door, the empty, unfurnished farmhouse makes me remember that I left at the pool the one living thing still residing with me—Kobi. Retracing to get him, I'm thinking I've got to furnish this place with sofas, tables, towels, TVs. Even so, it'll never compare in my kids' minds to the Ponderosa, the seven-thousand-square-foot, amenity-rich New Canaan, Connecticut, McMansion where the STBE is ensconced.

The rental is a seven-crumbling-fireplaces affair with, behind a bookcase, a reputed Underground Railroad hiding spot. That may make it quaint and mysterious to women, but it's just plain creepy to my kids. I'm having trouble, though, bringing myself to furnish it. To get myself walking down aisles reliving every acquisitive moment of my adult life, every one of my acts of purchase as I moved from hippie to worker, from shitty to well-paying job, from single to married, from young couple to parents, repurchasing everything that, over the past twenty-three years, I already searched out, price-compared, agonized over, found on sale, hauled home, opened, assembled, installed and, when I could afford a better one, threw out.

Back in the kitchen, Cara eyes me impatiently as I feed Kobi. She then playfully blocks my way to the oven, keeping me from setting it at 425 degrees for the roast. I know she's thinking I'm romancing her with cooking—though she doesn't need any—and I'm not. Putting out a good meal is just my way of proving to myself that I'm not completely drunk.

"I have something for you for an appetizer," she says, her words as smooth and round as her little Puerto Rican ass, the one she just now swivels and, dropping her skirt, rubs against me as she pulls my hands around and inside her thighs. I pull one away to set the oven, the other one, no longer in my control, plays with her as she arches her head back, administering the *coup de grâce*: a throaty moan in my ear.

I met Cara through Dinner's on Me, a dating system that preys on males with in-flight-magazine-story attention spans and I guess, like me, Internet dating stage fright. I was willing to pay almost any price—$1,400—for someone else to select women who wouldn't offend my sensitive ego by rejecting me out of hand, women who'd already said "yes" because, heh, dinner's on me.

DOM's intake is done by Suzy Cream Cheese from Greenwich, a nicely decanted, early fortyish ex-cheerleader type. Suzy is an attractant of indeterminate origin, with long blond hair and porcelain skin, a lady who, I guess, is what DOM's corporate honchos think relatively well-off, middle-aged guys like me want. Then you're turned over to their harem-master, a eunuch-seeming guy who leaves voice messages announcing himself as DOM's Hawart. He leaves the same message after every date, asking for feedback, enacting a script meant to project that DOM cares.

"Thusan," my first DOM date, is German. Marrying—and quickly divorcing—a GI stationed in some city I know I saw bombed in *The Rise and Fall of the Third Reich*, Thusan talks incessantly about her love of financial services, apparently a real *human* service to her.

"I help people understand zeir risk level. Zen I tailor zeir portfolio to zeir risk," she says, adding, as best I can understand, that there's nothing quite so exciting as "laddering bonds."

My second DOM setup calls herself Lily, which definitely isn't what she goes by back in Taiwan. Lily checks a big stack of FedEx flat-pack delivery boxes, then sashays towards me with that "Don't you dare stare at my flat Asian chest" look that makes me divert my attention to the Bloomingdale's "Big Brown Bag" she's kept with her.

"Shopping?" I ask.

"Sort of," I think she says, explaining in pulverized English that her factory in *Dongdung*, or *Guandung*, or some other mainland Chinese *dung*-place will, by early next week, produce thousands of knock-offs of these, the latest Bloomingdale's and Bergdorf Goodman designs, all to sell in Target and T.J. Maxx for pennies of what's charged for the original.

Third is a Russian lawyer built like a Stalingrad bunker. Fourth, a Pole looking for someone to finance her pierogi business. Fifth is a Lithuanian who, when she asks about my religion, and is told "nonpracticing Jew," physically recoils until I explain that I'm considered anti-Semitic because I can't stand what Israel does.

I have stopped answering Hawart's calls because, really, all I want to do is berate him for his agency misrepresenting that there's actually matchmaking occurring. It all seems scripted, stereotyped, certainly not tailored. Each so-called *match* is "a great girl" who loves "cooking and eating out," "dressing up and not," "going out on the town and staying in," "baseball and ballet," "reading," "theatre," "mainstream and off-beat movies" and, of course, "travel," as demonstrated by Hawart naming someplace airplanes fly where the woman has been. They all have a body of a definable build and measurable height and eyes and hair from one of Mendel's palettes. And each works in a major *sector*: "Financial Services," "Nonprofit," "IT," "Healthcare," "Telecommunications."

My most generous interpretation is that their matchmaking is just typecasting. Me, for example, just a former Wall Street lawyer who left to build and sell IT companies and, now retired, is ready to travel the world with his *special someone*. This crude characterization—whitewashing really—can't account for the bruises and blemishes bound to come through as people meet and the pancake makeup the matchmaker's applied wears off. I, for example, feel more like a lonely inmate than a former titan of industry. Gone are virtually all my relationships. Abandoned by all the couples who knew me during my marriage. No more business acquaintances, who disappeared when companies were sold. Heaps of brothers- and sisters-in-law, nieces and nephews on the STBE's side whom I've known for twenty-five years to whom, suddenly, I'm *persona non grata,* XXX-rated. Even gradually losing contact with my children because their stays with me are harder to negotiate than North Korean disarmament. You should see how fast these women turn dinner into "I only have time for coffee" when I let this cat out of the bag before ordering.

After a full boat of dates, all immigrants, I figure out DOM's real trip: they convince mainly foreign, financially obsessed women, that DOM supplies financially eligible guys—those who can afford $1,400 (versus online dating's twenty-two bucks a month) and the check for a risky dinner.

Finishing my sixth DOM dinner at *Pierre-Frank* in the West Village, I realize that Isabel, across the table, is my first DOMer who can open her mouth without alarming the INS. Though we're wrapping up dessert, I still don't know her last name; info that, during my dating hiatus, has moved from general to classified, from part of the introduction to being revealed only when the guy's provisionally accepted. A coded message: *semaphore*. Receiving her last name signifying her conclusion that nothing thus far suggests I'm a pervert or a stalker, deliberations on the final verdict—phone and address—ongoing.

Frankly, I understand why Isabel hasn't given me her last name yet; if I were her, I wouldn't give mine to someone thinking what I'm thinking.

I'm deconstructing her. Breaking her into little pieces like Jeffrey Dahmer. *Writes grant proposals for nonprofits. Paints for her soul. A little quirky but definitely left wing and into movies. Not condescending, self-impressed, or stuck-up. Beautiful white straight teeth tightly spaced like the blocks in the pyramids. A luscious oval mouth. Full, wide lips. Billowy long brown hair. Big, symmetrical blue eyes. Smooth skin. A full curvy body with Hepburn-like broad shoulders and breasts, though sweater-enhanced, still of good size.*

Maybe this cannibal-like thinking is what's making it hard for me to figure out if I'm attracted to her, the whole of people (to all but Jeffrey Dahmer) apparently more of an aphrodisiac than the sum of their parts.

We get out of the restaurant okay, though I'm a bit unstable as we walk to my truck. She tells me about her five cats, which I take as a warning of a cat-stenchy apartment. I swing across 23rd Street into the bus stop in front of the building she's pointing to. We smile. Sigh. It's quiet except for the traffic. Her face grows larger and, though I've noticed that faces often look nicer up close, hers gets edgier as she leans in, clamps me with her lips and pries mine apart with her tongue, shucking me like a starfish straddling a clam, her tongue seeking soft innards. Suddenly I understand why I'm having so much trouble figuring out what to do. I'm not feeling *it*, the *chemistry* governing predictable reactions that, incongruously, we use as a euphemism for what none of us understands.

Actually, I want to call Hawart and tell him to stop sending women *picked* because DOM has to refund my money if they don't send me on at least three dates a month. I want him to stop acting as if I'm so stupid that I believe someone there's actually thinking about who's compatible with me. And Hawart, next time, tell me something interesting. Tell me Thusan's "got bulimia and agoraphobia, but she's working on it." That Lily "has anger-management issues that make Russell Crowe look like a Zen master." That Ms. Russian lawyer is "so full of herself she makes Donald Trump look like a monk." That Ms. Pierogi "needs a guy who can put up with her inane chatter." That "though Ms. Lithuania likes being eaten, she has trouble reciprocating," meaning she's working on swallowing.

Home, an email arrives from Isabel saying that she "had a wonderful time" and hopes I feel likewise because "we have so much in common."

"Looking forward to getting together again," she says in a follow-up email, sheepishly apologizing for being "a bit forward," something to do with her "passionate nature" that makes it hard for her "to resist her feelings."

The next morning, another. This one wondering whether my silence means what she thinks it does and, if so, how I could write her off so quickly. How I could decide how I feel without us ever having "discussed us."

―――――

Cara, my current DOM setup, was the only one to yield something approximating a relationship. Cara's soft Puerto Rican accent was soothing during our first *dinner*, actually, heretically, a lunch I got drunk at a few weeks ago.

Cara is a nubile-looking thirty-five-year-old recent divorcee who runs the human resources department at some company. She's an upwardly mobile Puerto Rican with a Dunkin' Donuts franchise in Harlem, a deli she set her mother up in, and who knows what else churning out dough. She was raised in San Juan by her mother and grandmother. Her father, a businessman, died in an accident when she was quite young.

"You don't sound happy to hear from me," she says, calling me the day after our first date.

"Oh, ummm, how are you?" I say, remembering a cute woman, physically my type but personality-wise not making it, probably a candidate for my libidinal cocktail of Absolut that gets me squeezing into places I don't belong.

"I made empanadas," she said. "You said you like empanadas. Mine are *verrrrry* good." She abruptly stops laughing, apparently self-conscious. She offers to bring them by.

"When?" I ask.

"That's me turning into your driveway," she says, and, sure enough, there she is, coming around the maple tree just outside my kitchen window.

Her coat off, she looks like a schoolgirl. Maybe even a *Lolita*. Like the one who stripped to Leonard Cohen's "Everybody Knows" in the movie *Exotica*. The kind that the pervert lurking in every guy gets a hard-on over. I size her up at four-ten and not a wrinkle in her baby face.

Barely discernable breasts. White button-down blouse. Black-pleated, schoolgirl-type velour jumper squaring off over the blouse and turning into shoulder straps. Loafers.

"I thought you'd like this," she says, blessedly handing me a Rioja.

Lascivious impulses I haven't felt since I read *Lady Chatterley's Lover* by flashlight course through me. And there's no downside. Nothing at stake. No responsibilities. No implication for a failing marriage. Just people doing what they do.

I beat the wine to her lips. She moves closer, pressing her body into mine. Immediately, we're wrestling up the rear staircase, into the main bedroom, impatiently ridding ourselves of cloth claptrap, her unlatching my belt, me pushing her blouse buttons through their eyes.

She's small and tight and curly, with raisin-hue nipples that look warty. I decide to look at them when I'm trying to calm myself down.

She whispers that she hasn't had sex since her seven-year-old son was conceived, after which her husband, though sticking around, turned away. Way too much detail for me, but it does explain her squeals, which, coupled with her tugging on my ass to force me back inside her, makes me feel like a real man. With uncharacteristic assurance, I begin flipping her over. She says something about a down-tilted uterus making doggy-style painful—*way too much information, again*—so I continue as we are.

She's cooing, resting her head on my shoulder.

I'm about to say something I don't want to. Something provocative, like announcing in the Diamond District that I wouldn't be caught dead in human rights-abusing Israel.

I'm trying to staunch it, but it comes, like a sneeze gone too far.

"*Coño*," I say, quick and clipped, angry, like the Spanish kids I once tutored taught me, satisfied, like a Latino complimenting a whore.

Her eyelids wiggle, but don't open. I know she's heard this barrio Spanish word, the equivalent of "fuck," *coño* being a word I haven't thought of since I lived on New York's Lower East Side thirty years ago.

"*Coño*," I repeat, assuming she's simmering. Because that's what I think I mean for her to do, I drag it out.

"*Coño*," I say again, fast and sweet, smiling as she finally opens her eyes, showing she heard me say that I love her pussy more than her, an unnecessary, impolite, hurtful thing that I can't understand myself saying.

I don't understand it when she just nestles in closer, unwrapping the arm she's got lying across me, sliding it under the covers, taking my dick.

Then I get it. She's "*coñoing*" me, and I don't like it. I don't like being told that my dick is all she really wants. Why are we having this conversation? Why am I trying so hard to ruin this purely sexual relationship? Why isn't it appealing that she's saying she wants the same thing I do?

STUCK IN THE PASSING LANE

It's Friday, the day of the date with Antonio Banderas' ex-wife, Ms. Smart-Ditzy-Sweet. Her building, The Apthorp, occupies a block-square on New York's Upper West Side. It's a pre-World War I, twelve-story stone fortress with arched entranceways, a brass guard booth and a gardened interior courtyard. Judging from the mix of restored and old windows, it's being "converted," serfs being replaced by people who buy rather than rent their estates.

The doormen look like Buckingham Palace transplants, bronze-buttoned coats, gold-braid epaulets, tall enough to make me feel like I'm sitting. Asking for Rene Flanello, I catch one sneering, then nodding seemingly towards the other, who I think rolls his eyes. *Is she late on the rent?*

The doormen are silent and inactive, not phoning or buzzing or making any effort to deal with my presence. They make me feel like I'm asking to use the bathroom in a fancy restaurant that I'm not patronizing. Asking for Rene Flanello again, I realize that this nodding is more than just a pejorative moment between colleagues. I head where the doorman's head is directing me: towards a side wood door that looks like the medieval service entrance to Notre Dame.

The enchanting cloister-like effect of the building abruptly ends as I pass under an eave where tiled vaulted ceilings give way to low, peeling sheetrock. To my right is a heavy-looking oak door, short and slightly hidden, definitely where Quasimodo-like hunchbacks sneak in and out. The door looks punier as I get closer, turning from oak to simulated paneling with *trompe l'oeil*-painted grooves. The doorknocker rasps like a gavel on a card table.

Almost as I knock, she appears—leaning, glowering and, as she speaks, expectorating.

Her face, puffy and wrinkled, has weathered every single second of what I'd estimate to be its seventy-plus years. Her eyebrows are sketched, *hairless,* rising well beyond her eye ridges, each eyebrow now a dark, sinister parabola plotted across the wrinkles lining her forehead. Her cheeks are so heavily rouged that they look like triangular mesas, their sides descending abruptly to ears, eyes, the ravine giving rise to her nose. And her red, red lipstick, applied with a heavy, shaky hand, meanders from lips to skin and back, double-width in places, making her look like an insane clown or, I'm thinking, Bette Davis in *What Ever Happened to Baby Jane?*

But all I can think of right now is her dress, shiny and thin, like the cheap gold foil they wrap poinsettias in, the light glinting off the polyester, the long line of wrinkled cleavage suggesting sag, not size.

I'm fixated and stunned. My eyes water from a cloud of incense.

"Here," she says, shoving an old black-beaded purse into my hand. "See if ya can unsnag this while I finish up."

I cling to the bag so firmly that tiny black beads, tearing from the aged stringing, ping all over the hardwood floor. Yanking on the stuck zipper only increases the miniature hailstorm.

I know I should double over from some sudden onset, terminal-without-immediate-treatment ailment like dysentery. But I'm inexperienced, lacking that reflexive response. I'm trapped in her lair where she's too scary to offend. And her enthusiasm is so completely out of touch with the reaction she's engendering that I feel sad, unwilling to hurt her. So I make my way through hangings of giant bird feathers wired together, past a table covered with tarot cards and through billowing incense.

I don't see a refrigerator or toilet, so I'm guessing I'm in the living room, though there's nowhere to sit. Taxidermy sculptures cover two of the walls: eight-foot, dusty, wing-like structures with garish, ostrich-size feathers. A single floor lamp illuminates more dust than space, a Lilliputian meteor shower.

I hear her footsteps. The doctor returning with the syringe.

Les Routiers, unfortunately, turns out to be really French. Dark paneling. Fat sommelier toting a Bible-size wine list. One of those places that serves no course before its tectonic time. The *maître d'* is taking us towards a corner booth, one where I'll have to sit next to her, close, like eating in bed. I motion towards a free-standing table that will ensure a safe distance.

She's facing the front of the restaurant. So when the *maître d'* heads for the rear, I excuse myself and slip him a twenty behind her back, a bribe. I tell him to turn the food out fast, not make me hunt for martini refills and, with a tip-altering edge to my voice, "no dessert menus."

"I'll have the . . ." I say as I open the menu, hoping to keep the waiter at our table and move the process along.

"Doesn't *monsieur* want to hear the specials?" he asks, describing about ten dishes with intolerable specificity.

"*Et le poisson du jour c'est loup de mer. Loup est un poisson française proche de votre sea bass mais avec—*"

"*Je veux le poisson,*" she interrupts, precipitating a torrent of "Fwench" between them the likes of which I haven't heard since I struggled through some classy French film that Netflix mistakenly delivered without subtitles.

"*Et vous, monsieur?*" he asks me after she finishes ordering.

"*Je veux le lapin,*" I say, the martini loosening me up.

Having heard my words in French, she starts spouting French faster than the Vichy government turned in Jews. She pauses and leers; her reaction, I assume, to me not answering her questions.

The food arrives as I insisted, quickly, which makes me feel better, like I have at least some vestige of control. I'm exploring mine, rabbit over starch and veggies in a fashionably indented plate. She's using her fork to make fast work of hers, mashing fish, beets and potatoes into a lumpy mush that she rolls into balls like I've seen African dung beetles do with elephant shit on the Discovery Channel. "Try this," she says, plopping one of her boluses in the middle of my plate.

Three, maybe four martinis later I'm enveloped in my own silence, comfortable saying nothing, though it makes her look like she's jabbering to herself.

The *maître d'* clears the dishes and then, true to what I bribed him for, conveniently forgets the dessert menus. When she asks about dessert, he claims that the people swooning over crème brûlée, apple tart and warm chocolate cake at the adjacent table got the last of them, an obvious lie that, rising, making my apologies and leaving, I don't wait for her to challenge.

The only way I can stop Cara's unannounced drop-bys is to meet at her house, which I leave right after sex. I drink on the ride over and while there, and stumble out. I realize that I'm drinking so much to get over the shame I feel about this relationship, the shame being entirely misplaced because sex obviously is enough for her, and it's all I've agreed to.

I watch my email ambivalently, hoping for—and dreading—a note from Cara breaking the stalemate between my heart, which doesn't seem to be able to treat someone this way, and my dick, which lusts for it. No matter what I do—even refusing to meet Cara's son, her mother, her friends—she still meets me at the door in a sheer nightgown, warning me after sex that, because we don't use condoms, I better not "*coño*" anyone else without telling her, which I promise to.

The last time, a few days ago, I left her house so drunk that I didn't even excuse myself, my penalty being the speeding ticket I got on the way home. My quiet politeness saved me from being breathalyzed and a slam-dunk DUI. Driving away, I decided to stay away, though not for any reason I can figure.

All I can think of is something my father told me when I was a teenager about to leave on my first date.

"Remember," he said, "she's somebody's sister."

UNNATURAL SELECTION

I FINALLY WRANGLE A SCHEDULE from the STBE for sharing time with the kids. Now I *really* have to furnish the place.

I find a 20 percent off coupon in the mailbox for Bed Bath & Beyond, which seems like *the* place to get everything that makes homes habitable. It's almost lunchtime. I want to drink, and I don't want to fill carts and then load and unload the truck, unwrap, unpack, hang up, put away and assemble, though imagining doing all this fills me with a sense of purpose, like sitting at a desk all day used to make me feel like I actually accomplished something. I wonder if I need to join the fraternity of working folks fooling themselves that being at a job all day means their lives are meaningful. *No,* I think. I worked all my life to achieve the one thing I know I have—financial independence. Chugging some vodka, my desire to drink thanks my twisted hubris.

I find my way to the Bed Bath & Beyond parking lot where, in the rush to get a cart and get through the too-slow-opening automatic door, I trip and fall backwards, and into my lap drops a vibrating body massager.

"Are you okay?"

The hand I grab belongs to a henna-haired Marlo Thomas *That Girl* lookalike who asks if she can help as she raises me, moving my hands to the cart handle like I'm being returned to my walker.

Her red polo shirt, embroidered *Bed Bath & Beyond*, is so tightly tucked that her breasts pop out like little figs under a taut sheet.

"Looking for something in particular?"

"I've got a whole house to do," I say, adding "Irene," which I'm reading off her nametag.

She's asking me questions about what I need, about lists and things, but I'm not answering because I'm stuck struggling not to be smitten with this young thing. I see signs everywhere that seem to be reading my mind: *Personal Care, Lubricated, Scented, Extra-Sensitive, Foamy, Refreshing*.

"How about starting with the bedrooms?" she asks, walking ahead, motioning with her finger for me to follow. I fall in line, eyes riveted on her ass swishing like a pendulum from a tiny waist. She drums her fingers on boxes of blenders, hangers, dishes, garbage cans, pot sets, subliminally signaling, I think, what I should buy, piles of which divide the originally ample aisle into two barely passable straits. I knock down a gumball machine box. That gets me wondering whether a gumball machine goes with the brown corduroy sectional with pop-up cup holders and footrests that I just had delivered from Bob's Discount Furniture, a place that caters to people like me who need delivery the second their credit card clears.

"What about these?" I'm pointing to the pillow bins behind her.

She points to signs explaining the types of pillows. Trying to seem attentive, I read these essays about firmness and allergens and fillings and foams. I squeeze the one she offers me like I think I'm supposed to, then cup it between my shoulder and head to show that I care about what she's saying.

"That one is good for neck support," she says.

"Neck support," I repeat, envisioning propping her up in a way that I'd like, fool that I am. She's barely post-teen, and I'm thinking like a guy drinking too much or, just possibly, so insecure that just about every attractive woman is a ballot-holder in my secret referendum about me.

"How many?"

"Ten," I say, figuring she's figuring four for me and two each for the rest of the beds, counting beds leading to counting children, leading to her reeling about how many I have. I'm thinking she probably wants some herself, something this now-regretful owner of a STBE-sponsored vasectomy can't give.

The cart's instantly replaced with another and another, as four bedrooms of comforters, pillow cases and sheets, and a houseful of other items, disappear into shopping carts that we fill like ore buckets at the mother lode, my Bed Bath & Beyond accessorista motioning towards items, me obsequiously nodding.

"Girls?"

"Yes."

"They'll need curtains, hangers, toiletries, hairdryers, towel hooks, mirrors, face towels, lamps, some cute throw pillows for the beds."

I return from a reconnaissance mission for toilet brushes that she sends me on. She's filling carts like they're catch basins in a torrent; consumer goods, soap, conditioners, shampoos, *feminine* stuff, hair brushes, hairdryers, pink-canned shaving cream, purple-handled throwaway shaving blades. But what I want more than anything is for her to wrap her arms around me like I'm a pristine box of something great, put me in her cart, pack me in her trunk, take me home, unwrap, unpack and assemble me. But to her I'm just a twenty-dollar coffee table cube with reversible game tops and ashtrays that double as cheese bubblers for fondue—useless junk.

"You cook?" she asks, dropping a grapefruit knife into a new cart.

"Had to," I say, pausing. "Married a feminist."

"Feminist?" she asks, her question giving me a near-death experience except that it's my future passing before me. I see myself explaining everything to these young women I'm attracted to: that the Vietnam War wasn't a trade dispute; that ice cubes once had to be broken out of trays; that being drafted didn't always mean having a shot at playing for the Knicks.

"Do you do set up?"

"Only in-store assembly," she says, ignoring my flirt.

"I mean help me set up at home."

"First get home." She points outside, where it's raining hard.

"I've got an open pickup."

"No problem. Just wait," she instructs, pressing her card into my hand.

Maybe I need a card. But saying what? I used to be stuff you could put on a card. Businessman. Road warrior. Uncle. Cook. Gardener. Homework helper. Light bulb changer. Toilet unclogger. Cable TV/Internet fixer. Bug killer. Vacation planner. But now I'm ex all that. I know. I'll have a card saying I'm ex-rated.

Irene appears with three guys carrying rolls of plastic wrap, enough to encase a cabin cruiser.

"Bring your truck under that overhang," she says. There, they go at it, stuffing fifteen cartloads of stuff into the back bay, then shrink-wrapping over and under until the truck's as impervious as a body bag.

With the kids not coming until next week, and Cara finished, I'm lonely, almost suicidal in my farmhouse haven where I'm trying to put bookends around my drinking. I'm trying to fill my life with diversions like wake-up rides on the StairMaster, fixing a radiator heat valve that's stuck open, working in the garden my kids and I built around a Westport, Connecticut homeless shelter. There, working drunk, I nearly whack a designer-clad passerby who, mistaking me for someone working for his dormitory cot, offers me half the minimum wage to mow her lawn. I take late afternoon walks with Kobi off-leash in the "town forest," about two hundred acres of overgrown, streamlined fields where, if I don't pack any booze, I don't drink.

More than anything, I'm hoping to be saved by a life-altering experience. Something that lifts me out of this swampy miasma of unappealing relationships, far from the panacea I expected when I left a quarter century of marriage behind. What am I doing? Answering ads from women much further from their primes than they let on? Lurching from one Hawart-inspired date to another? Oh it's gotten me dating, even laid. And with Hawart doing the choosing, I don't have to worry about being passed over for anything having to do with me, like a photo in my cyberprofile, or how I describe myself, or an email that a cyber-recipient doesn't find appealing. That sort of rejection will leave me torturing myself, pining over a relationship I've never had but feel I've lost. Too risky. My ego might not survive it.

STUCK IN THE PASSING LANE

Decades ago, the prospect of pain in dating wasn't as great because of the limited possibilities of finding someone. Back then, the ideal woman had to emerge from the sea. Bo Derek in cornrows inexorably rising with the sexy rest of her from the ocean floor. To find her, you cruised beaches and bars scanning for beauties. In the rare instances you found them, they weren't available: ringless possibilities you talked up at parties only to be introduced to husbands grateful for someone babysitting their wives; bars filled with babes with absent but existing boyfriends; colleges filled with women waiting for anyone—but you—to ask for their phone numbers; isolated, accidental encounters with exuberant women enticing until they mention fiancés.

But while I struggled through my married decades of dating limbo, online dating sites like Match and eHarmony and ChristianMingle and Yahoo personals were obliterating all this, putting the mating process on steroids by stripping it of chance. Now, with the push of a button, thousands of eager women, all available and conveniently marshaled and sorted, can be marching towards you like the army of electronic aliens in the arcade game Space Invaders. They're arrayed six or twelve or twenty to a page, depending on how much you want to see at first glance. It's a constant online meeting of Lonely Hearts Club Anonymous, every pop-up participant announcing "I'm available, come get me," the perceived prospect for pleasure exponentially increasing along with the opportunity for pain.

But these days I think I'm more of a guy girls may want. My car's a late model with same-color fenders and a working heater, able to come to a full stop without yanking the emergency brake, and with ample space where a couple of kilos of pot used to be. I'm well-traveled and keep my body somewhat toned. I'm relatively rich and retired, having just sold my IT business. And I have three laptops ready to announce my love objects' emails throughout the eclectic farmhouse that's replaced the twenty-five-dollar-a-week basement I rented the last time around.

And actually, I've been pushing my nose under the tent, dipping a toe. Fed up with the matchmaking service Dinner's on Me, I'm checking out women's profiles on Match.com while my profile there remains safely hidden. I've even compiled a file of my "Favorites": the profiles and photos of women whom I'll contact upon my as-yet unscheduled debut.

I'm in the last throes of carefully reviewing my Match profile, like you're supposed to do with your SAT answers when you finish early. I tone down all the stuff about my kids, making it seem that I love but can do without them. The rephrasing ensures that both kinds of women will want me—those wanting fathers for their kids, and those wanting one to themselves. I eliminate phrases like *soul mate* and *the woman I'll spend my next quarter century with* so I'll appeal both to those wanting love and those just wanting *it* Thursdays during lunch. I check my photos. Me humorously holding plastic flowers. Me petting a camel in the desert. A well-produced headshot.

My finger's on the button that switches my account to "Everyone Can See You," which reveals my profile, exposing me to tens of thousands of women using Match, but I chicken out temporarily, going instead to my Favorites file. These women, I notice, mostly use the opportunity of their profiles to describe, not themselves, but their *gimmes*—what the man for them should look like, be like, think like, dress like, sometimes even smell like. Most seem to want a Richard Gere clone into whom Frankenstein's surgeon has transplanted Albert Einstein's brain, Bill Gates's affinity for making money, Billy Crystal's sense of humor, Fred Astaire's dancing prowess and Valentino's bedside manner.

I linger over a widow, wondering if she'll be less jaded, unlikely to complain about her dearly departed ex, not triggering me doing the same about my live one. Then a beautiful thirty-two-year-old divorcee who describes her desire for children with such biological urgency that each passing second seems to cut as it ticks. I know I'll have to reverse my vasectomy for her, not to mention put up again with little kids.

I notice that the prettier they are, the more willing I am to overlook telltale signs of them being difficult or incompatible with my tastes. Can't write? Can't spell? Thinks the *New York Post* qualifies as reading material? No matter if you're hot. I'm considering a beautiful woman with messed blond hair broadly smiling from atop a rock by a cool mountain lake, though she begins every sentence with some variation of "And you also better be… or don't contact me." Heh, maybe she's just recovering from a string of bad dates.

Then I notice a woman I moved to Favorites a few days ago, one calling herself "Sugarfilly" whose pictures show her draped across the Metropolitan Museum's steps, her slinky, high black-leather boots disappearing into the tiny area that's all that her short red miniskirt leaves to the imagination. She says she looks younger than the forty she's checked off. A self-described "former model" returning from "running with horses in Arizona," her "burrs," according to her personal statement, needing some gentle but firm "combing" by "sophisticated, sensitive back-East hands."

It's too much for me. Faster than Angelina Jolie's *first* donned his condom when she gave him the high sign, I click "Everyone Can See You," making myself visible, taking this guy with a blank domino profile out for a spin. Then I wait for my little envelope icon signifying incoming messages to light up like a telethon phone bank.

But nothing happens.

I decide to search for myself to make sure I'm "Visible."

I search as a "Woman Seeking Men" between "53" and "53," between "5'6"" and "5'6"," within five miles of "06840." *Presto chango*, there's me, plus the competition, a bunch of much more virile-looking guys. I shut the search down, feeling inadequate.

With nothing happening, I decide to take the bull by the horns.

"Hey, Sugarfilly," I type, but only after deleting, because she doesn't seem to be the motherly kind, the reference in my profile to my three teenage daughters, and increasing my height, which, in fairness, I compensate for by slightly reducing my age.

"Can't believe I haven't run into a beauty like you at the Sanctuary," I write, referring to Phoenix's most expensive spa. This hopefully libido-luring sentence is designed to convey that I've got good taste, love travel and have the checkbook to support both—a pheromonic trifecta.

The longer my self-described burr-picker-seeker doesn't answer, the more her image haunts me, her silence becoming an unremitting ache. I seek relief by writing to perhaps more appropriate women closer to my age, around my height, some once married, others presently separated, many with children, even teenagers. I approach those "Active within 24 Hours," a sign the Help section says means she's actively looking, hasn't given up. The silence continues, the passage of time amplifying pain.

Sugarfilly shocks me with an answer. Her name is Christina. She likes my profile and will contact me in a few days when she arrives in New York. I thank her and tell her to let me know when. On the strength of all this, I introduce her to relatives and friends, showing them her sexy pictures, her classy web profile, her promising note.

It's been exactly a week since I heard from Sugarfilly. I'm doing everything I can to keep from checking every minute for an email from her, for something announcing her arrival or explaining her silence or delay. To distract myself, I unpack, unwrap, assemble, hang and distribute everything I bought at Bed Bath & Beyond. This self-imposed delay in checking for her email feels like holding off an orgasm.

But every time I break down and check, there's nothing. So much time passes and so much nothing happens that I'm now avoiding embarrassing questions from people I'd assured that Sugarfilly would soon be dangling from my arm.

Worse, I'm tortured by a void she's left. We've already hugged together many nights in my dreams. And her accepting presence has filled my otherwise empty afternoons. No longer able to conjure her up, I'm left with pain far less imaginary than the person who's disappeared.

To break out, I decide to be even more particular, to write earnestly and attentively, and to freely rebrand myself. I parse women's profiles for *their* interests that I can say or make believe we share—the same *place* we vacationed, the same *book* we read, the same *profession* we worked in—pretenses for saying they look hot and that I hope we can meet.

I invite the blond-haired, blue-eyed basketball aficionado to a New York Knicks game to which I don't yet have tickets. I expound about contemporary authors I haven't read—Wallace, DeLillo, Foer, Hazzard, Didion—to the beautiful avid reader. With stories of places like Patagonia, where I've never been, I romance the Connecticut headhunter who loves traveling.

I'm Cyrano de Bergerac fronting for myself.

I CAN'T TAKE ME ANYWHERE

It's Memorial Day weekend and, rather than picking out a beach house and planning a summer of STD-free sex, I'm sitting at my desk wrapped in my bedspread shaking with the flu.

My You've Got Mail envelope flickers showing two new Match emails that I open with the same expectation as scratching a lottery card. The first is from a woman who thanks me for writing and, after saying that I seem like a nice guy, concludes that I probably don't recognize that she's my thirteen-year-old's science teacher who I recently met at a parent-teacher conference. The second follows a similar arc. This one's the rabbi at the synagogue where the same daughter recently was bat mitzvahed, leaving me wondering if I'm the guy in *Memento* who's lost his short-term memory or, as I believe is the case, there's no resemblance between the decked-out babe I wrote to and the chubby Hebrew National emissary who just welcomed my daughter to manhood.

One hand clutching the Absolut, I'm about to head up to bed to drown my shivers with booze, but as I move to log off, the screen pops with a You've Got a Wink. This is the Internet dating version of a hunky construction worker whistle.

Though my experience with winks is that they're usually from women who need to make the first move because their looks are of limited appeal, I click anyway and, surprisingly, Match brings up a photo of a very cute brown-haired, blued-eyed woman calling herself Funnybunny.

I'm tempted to reply right away, start the flow of information, try teasing out something about her, but then I take a better look at her picture, a head and chest shot that I double in size, the maximum enlargement Match allows.

What are those? I wonder, focusing on twin saucer-like UFOs hovering in front of her chest—twin melons that can't be what I think they are, if only because they shouldn't haven gotten past Match's censors.

I'm suspicious. A guy at the tennis club told me about hoax women. Not transvestites, but beautiful young surfer girls whose photos guys put up on the Internet along with risqué profiles, all to toy with the horny old perverts who respond. I parse her profile using all my Evelyn Wood speed-reading tools to get to the important words, the nouns.

"43," "Divorced," "New York, New York." *Sounds okay.* "Professional," "Arts," "Theatre" and "Travel." *Reasonable.*

"Looking for long-term relationship." Seems a bit incongruous given the photo but, hey, she's leading with her best feature: fabulous, flaunt-worthy tits. "Twin five-year-old boys."

Toggling to the photo, I focus on the top of the spheres. On close inspection, they're not tits. They're the tops of the heads of her twin five-year-olds. Though I wonder about the thought process, or lack thereof, that leads to showing your toddlers to the cyber-dating world, since she's cute and winked at me, and I'm now convinced she's not a fake surfer girl, I reply, noting that, with twins of my own, I know how hard it must be bringing them up as a single mom.

Instantly, she emails back, asking how I ended up in Connecticut and whether I intend to remain up there. I ask if she's a native New Yorker and what she likes to do in her spare time. She says she's pretty busy with her as-yet unspecified job. She asks whether I'm really retired and, if so, what I do to keep busy. I tell her that I'm thinking about moving to the city at some point, and that I keep busy with charitable work which, to a modest extent, I do.

And so it goes. All day Saturday until midnight. Sunday too. Like the only thing we've got to do is email each other, a two-person daisy chain of bantering, usually hourly, sometimes quicker, often ignoring one another's questions, sticking to the superficial shallow end, avoiding anything meaningful, such as why we're divorced, what our respective choices in exes was about. It's a giant dose of cyber-foreplay, or maybe something like gas, what you have to pass to get comfortable, which, here, means getting her phone number and then arranging the meeting to perform the ceremonial laying on of eyes.

The flu, the booze, the snot, the cough, they're all conspiring to erode my voice, which now is so hoarse that I'm delaying asking for her phone number because the sick and old image this voice will project isn't what I'm going for. Sunday night, I cave and ask her if she wants to speak. Two hours later, her telephone number arrives.

I leave a message that I think is relaxed and not too polished, like I'm a sophisticated, worldly guy who, though humble, doesn't much need to do this sort of thing. Since I'm hoarse, which is making me even more self-conscious, I make a joke, saying that I must sound like Kate Hepburn, hoping that sounds cute, attractively self-effacing.

Then nothing. I mean *nothing*. No call back Sunday night. No call back Memorial Day Monday. Resounding, excommunicating silence. Nothingness so astonishing that I actually call myself from my landline to make sure my cell phone's working. And like a spy, I track her on Match, determining that she's "Active," meaning she's alive, logging in, looking around, hour-by-hour, just not answering me.

Something inside just won't accept this. It grows into a need that enlarges into an irresistible impulse to violate the *numero uno* Don Juan rule of dating: never, ever seem desperate. Unable to resist, I pick up the phone and leave another message, pissing away my last drop of that great aphrodisiac: indifference.

It's Tuesday morning. My fever's gone, along with the shakes and chills that once seemed inescapable. Not so, though, the needy, abandoned, rejected feeling that Ms. I-Gave-You-My-Phone-Number-But-I'm-Not-Calling-You-Back left me with. To the contrary, she's rekindled memories of the gnawing, lovesick, crush-driven pain that dogged my adolescence and, like then, is inescapable.

So I'm thinking how to fan the flames, or at least blow on the embers. Perhaps if I dig deeper I can confirm that, rather than rejecting me, she's medically stricken, perhaps paralyzed, possibly comatose, maybe even dead.

So I plug her phone number into Switchboard.com, a reverse directory that promises to find names for listed numbers.

Presto! "Charlotte Ripley."

I plug Charlotte Ripley into Google and, presto, more hits than the first day of Paris Hilton's blow job video.

What the hell is this about?

Reading, I see that Little Ms. Popular is a costume designer. But not just any costume designer. She's the award-winning costume designer who designed the costume that a certain someone wore during the infamous 2004 Super Bowl XXXVIII halftime show, the costume that got somebody inducted into the pantheon of celebrities who've publicly revealed their nipples. According to the articles, since then, it seems that Ms. Charlotte's been holed up with lawyers suing various parties on her behalf for the hundreds of thousands of dollars she's allegedly owed for the costumes for the whole show. Apparently, she contends that it was just a minor oversight, and not gross negligence, to have engineered it so that Justin Timberlake removed a red-lace bra in the course of ripping off Janet Jackson's bodice. There are hundreds of comments on how absurdly thoughtless it is for an experienced costume designer not to have done better, including many analogies between babies and baths, and bras and bustiers. These websites are like car crashes; I don't want to look but I can't stop. I continue exploring this woman's persona and, as I do, my need to drink, which has been tempered the past few days by the flu and, probably, my obsession with her, burns through.

What am I looking for? I think as, helplessly, I continue digging, discovering the name of the design firm where she works. I go on their website, accessing her starchy-smiling picture to which I raise my first Absolut since her initial wink. Why am I so obsessed with her, someone I don't know one bit? Didn't I learn anything from Sugarfilly? Is Internet dating my own particular hell, or is it an equal-opportunity torturer, snaring just about everyone this way? And did Funnybunny pick me especially for this treatment, like there's a sign on my back saying "Toy with Me," or does she do this to everyone?

I'm trying to end this fixation, to close the book on her. The evidence suggests that she plays a bit fast and loose with clothing. Maybe she does the same with relationships, acting like she wants one though she has absolutely no intention of ever crossing the cyber-gap. But I can't stop thinking that it's something about the voice message I left, my tone, a phrase I used, something about my face that became apparent only when she enlarged it. I'm hooked on her line and, though she's obviously got an edge, a loose screw, Absolut's the only thing freeing me.

I try to stop thinking about her, but I can't accept that I'm just a short, balding centerfold to her. Maybe I can do something to entice her back? Something that rekindles whatever it was that got her to wink. With my neediness hovering, I feel like the lonely old lady in the French restaurant, the one who thought lobbing food boluses onto my plate was connecting. That's who I am now. *Pathetic.*

I make some calls until I find a florist a block from her office. I give them her name and work address and my credit card. I tell them that her note, the one they'll deliver with the two-dozen tulips I'm ordering, should say, "Thanks for a wonderful Memorial Day Weekend." Hanging up, I'm fantasizing about the pleased look on her face when the tulips arrive. I enjoy that image until I start thinking that someone who's probably receiving bushels of hate mail from Janet Jackson and Justin Timberlake fans (not to mention Moral Majority and Jerry Falwell followers), probably has the FBI on speed dial.

———————

"How did you find me?" says her email that arrives three hours later. While the jury's out about this in my mind, I'm getting the feeling, if only from the brevity of her response and the lack of a phrase saying something like "Thank you," that my tulips have *not* had the desired effect.

I'm writing an email explaining exactly how I did it, including apologizing if I've offended her. I'm also thinking about my liability. I've got no idea what laws there are on this kind of thing. It'd be just my luck that there's some recently passed He Just Won't Go Away law that some creative, shameless lawyer could claim protects women from just about anything that bothers them, including unsolicited tulips.

Though I make full disclosure, enveloping it in a contrite and circumspect response, her attitude doesn't soften; like a ricochet, I get back an exposition on "Internet Dating Etiquette." About a quarter way through, I realize that it's just the same thing retold about twenty different ways: *While, generally, anything goes, don't bother someone whose words or actions or lack of actions say they don't want to be bothered by you.* I skim the rest, which seems like more of the same, plus citations to legal opinions on privacy rights, what constitutes stalking, what happens to those who do it.

Being a lawyer, I recognize the format of this document. It's a legal memorandum. I'm imagining a lunch break during which Ms. Funnybunny mentions to her battalion of lawyers that she needs protection. She's being inundated with unsolicited tulips and, if they don't do something fast, she may soon find herself bombarded with chocolates, jewelry, theatre tickets, maybe even lifetime Botox. A junior lawyer, probably a recent female Harvard law graduate, is assigned the task. Ecstatic to be doing pro-women's rights, domestic-violence preventing, date-rape-avoiding work, by morning the kid's produced the legal memo that I've been sent.

I rehydrate my sense of humor with Absolut. How offensive could a bunch of tulips be? And she created this problem, sending out mixed signals, making me think she's looking for a relationship when all she wants is to wake up to a bunch of ego-boosting emails from guys salivating over her ambiguous titty-twin photos.

And what about those titty-twins? What kind of woman trolls for men using suggestively placed headshots of her kids as bait? What woman wants guys she's toying with and irritating to know what her kids look like? But maybe they're not her kids. Maybe they're just Photoshopped. Maybe she's as altogether fake as all the corporate and governmental outrage claiming that seeing a nipple on a well-developed breast is a national catastrophe.

But, really, honestly, I'm beginning to see that how I respond to these people is the problem. Perhaps I'm just too easily hooked, too open, too vulnerable. I'm thinking about resigning myself to being alone, which is looking better and better, just Absolut and me.

MISS-STEPPING STONES

The phone rings. It's the STBE. I reach for more Absolut, something to smooth the jarring transition from a nightmare about someone I don't know to one generated by someone I do.

"They asked me to call," STBE says, forgoing pleasantries, or at least her usual "It's me." Not a good sign.

"Well, why don't you put one of them on?"

"They don't feel comfortable confronting you."

"Confronting?"

"They're afraid to express themselves to you."

"But they tell me to go to hell all the time."

"You're stealing their voices."

I remember this "stealing voices" accusation, what she accused me of having done to her every time she acted angry but refused to explain why. The indictment, she'd assert, was a consequence of my repeated prior offense of "not respecting boundaries," a crime amply defined in the self-help books piled on her side of the bed.

"Okay. What is it?"

"They've got a lot of homework."

"And?"

"They don't want to stay over."

"Okay."

"And tomorrow's Photo Day."

"Guess we should order two sets," I say, reminding myself that, by moving out, not getting the mail, I'm now dependent on her for knowing stuff. I'll have to find ways to keep up on my own. School conferences. Marching band performances. Student directory listings. Dance recitals. Horse shows. And Passover's coming. I always cook for Passover. For her whole family. Grandparents, uncles, aunts, cousins, friends. What's going to happen with that?

"Tomorrow night's the eighth grade dance."

"I wish I knew about this stuff," I say.

"If you'd been driving them around all these years, filling out the forms, you'd know," she says.

This, I know, is the new script, the secret history of her twenty-three years of extraordinary rendition in a gilded prison from which victims tortured with wealth and freedom emerge with PTSD, debilitated for life.

"Come on. I was cooking when you were driving. We divided the labor. It's just that I'm not there now."

"I'm busy. And the kids are busy. And they don't want to cart their stuff over to dress for pictures and the dance."

"Okay."

"And they've got too much homework to come for dinner."

"I'll make dinner short. Please put one of them on."

"So you can badger them?"

"Badger? Look, one of us had to move out. Why can't you help with this?"

"Tonight they're staying here doing homework."

"But at least let me schedule," which is all I get out before she hangs up.

I down more Absolut to calm my sense of emergency about yet another thwarted effort to have the kids stay with me, acclimate to their dad's new house. If I'd moved out earlier, I think, when they were younger, more easily ingrained, the transition would have been easier. But, desperate for them not to have to deal with a broken home like I did, I stayed on, probably way too long.

I take out the clothes that I bought for them at the Gap, Banana Republic and Anthropologie—what I thought I'd be giving them tonight. I worry about my ill-informed guesses about preferences in tops, jackets, sweaters and sweatshirts, colors and styles. I ineptly refold them, trying to arrange them attractively for when the girls do come, the mere act of doing something for them making me feel better, their continued absence, worse.

I call a company to order video games, attractive nuisances, something stupid but unique, as it's one pleasure they don't have at the Ponderosa: Pac-Man, Space Invaders, a thing called Mega with 400 games including Hooters and Solitaire. I distribute to the girls' rooms the miniature Bose sound systems and small, thick Kurdish rugs I bought. Now maybe they'll feel more at home because they can do their homework the way they do it at the Ponderosa, lying on the carpeting in their bedrooms, music blasting.

My cell phone rings.

"Dad?" says my daughter Nori, one of my sixteen-year-old twins.

"Honey, how are you?"

"Okay. I hope you don't mind. I ordered some furniture for my room online."

"Mind? Absolutely not. I'm happy. Is it being shipped here?"

"Yeah."

"Okay, we'll put it together, well, together. I'm getting good at that. Did you decide which room you want?"

"The all-the-way-upstairs one."

"The attic? That'd be my choice too. I'll figure out some way you can turn the light on from the bottom of the stairs. Did I tell you about the video games?"

"Dad?"

"What, honey?"

"Why don't you invite all of us over for dinner?"

"Everyone, including your mother?"

"Uh . . . yeah. I think it'll help."

"But—"

"And Dad, make sure the spiders are gone by next week."

"I—"

"Love you. Miss you. Bye."

Nori, challenging, as in dating older boys and, yes, so caring. Her call is like a tranquilizer and, with it, though I'm still warily eyeing the laptops, my inbox still empty, I am calming down.

"Remember me?" says the cell phone voice, one that reminds me how hard I tried to stay married, and how short a time it's been, just a couple of months, since I moved out.

"Francesca . . . from the Y. Remember me?" she repeats.

How could I forget my swimming companion, the one who kept me moving in the lane reserved for the fastest swimmers? So wonderfully curvaceous. So anatomically incorrect for water sports favoring the thin and sleek, yet moving through the pool with the speed and grace of an undulating dolphin and executing her flip turns like the star of an Esther Williams aqua musical. Keeping my head underwater for as long as I could when we passed, trying to get the best view of her beautifully endowed, flowing body, I almost hit the wall on occasion. A Milanese of Jewish extraction whose family immigrated here when she was a teenager, she was even more striking out of the pool, tall, with auburn hair and green eyes. She was my only romance during my marriage, one that began about a year ago, just after the STBE and I decided for the first time to divorce.

Francesca and I still dwelled in houses also occupied by our STBEs—her impending divorce being more advanced, deeply within the bickering-recrimination stage. We had no place to go, so we met at the Greenwich YMCA, often quitting before we hit the water, then making out where we could—hand jobs in movie theatres, blow jobs in backseats, carnal activity in the densely forested Mianus River Park in nearby Stamford. All my systems were *go, go, go*, as long as we were having sex where it was risky and unpermitted, conditions so intense that, looking back, lascivious excitement must have displaced paralyzing guilt.

It emerged when we arranged an evening together in a local motel, our first unhurried, unworried opportunity to make love. But, once alone with her, I couldn't wait to leave. It felt claustrophobic, the difficulty of dealing with that feeling compounded by having to try my best to hide my escapist impulse. Though I didn't think anything could, it felt worse than the ride home after our first kiss months earlier, my first passionate encounter in over twenty years with someone other than my wife. Guilty for saving myself at the expense of my kids, suffused with a profound sense of failure, a kiss that I expected to open new doors instead slammed one shut. Despite Francesca's valiant efforts, this motel time together that we'd both looked forward to was a failure; my dick, an emotional barometer, lost pressure.

I ended the relationship with Francesca when my STBE agreed to try again to stay together, this time using couples therapy. I'm not proud of it, but I left open with Francesca the possibility of continuing. Obviously having more self-control over her feelings than I did, she, able to call something illicit when it had become so, refused. She also felt duped. It had taken months to convince her to have an affair with me. Her profound hesitation, ultimately well-founded, was that she didn't want to involve herself with someone still married, despite the contradiction of her situation being as-yet unconcluded. She worried, in retrospect correctly, that I was unreliably new to the idea of divorce.

But I'd been honest with Francesca, the relationship with her having been forged based on the truth as I then knew it. Though I was being equally candid about my renewed efforts to save my marriage, that couldn't have been much of a salve to her. My openness probably is the reason I hadn't heard from her in over a year.

"The most wonderful blow jobs ever," I say, a stupid thing I think, kind of in the vein of saying *coño* to Cara, except I like Francesca as a person and, frankly, I'm already fighting fantasies about why she's called.

"Really?" she says.

"Really," I say, relieved, already thinking of the day she knelt down behind the bathrooms at the beach, directing me to plunge into her beautiful, inviting mouth, telling me not to pull out though I was on the verge of not being able to help myself, a precipice that I dutifully went over, a first for me.

While she doesn't say she's missed me, and we don't arrange to meet, she follows up with more phone calls and then emails, the two of us, for several days, graphically reliving our months of courtship: our kissing sessions by the pool behind her house, the soups I made her, the hot sex in exposed places, the dangers we assumed as we celebrated our impending emancipations. Though I'm dying to make sweet butternut squash soup for her like I used to, I'm patient. I don't push. I wait to see. The hopes I harbor expand with each communication.

The phone LCD shows it's Mitch, the bartender at my local watering hole and, at one time, my personal trainer. Mitch would be a dead ringer for Bruce Willis if only he had more of Willis's humor and puckishness, and was a bit more engaging and less macho. Three mornings a week, he dutifully met me at the gym at five thirty, pumped and ready to violate my one early-morning workout rule: no talking. Incessantly jabbering about interpersonal and financial issues, often reading me notes from his leather, zippered pad-folio about newfangled product ideas he thought could become winners, Mitch made me his confidant, shrink, business-idea-reality-tester and friend.

"How're you doin'?" From the tinny sound of his voice, I know I'm on speakerphone.

"Tennis Thursday?" I ask.

"You didn't confirm."

"Confirm? When did we start confirming?"

"Sorry, I'm playing with someone else. But I'm going to get my hair colored. Wanna come?" Mitch asks, ignoring my question, probably still in his morning haze, just out of the first of his several daily showers, or concentrating on grooming himself with his most recently acquired Sharper Image hair clipper. Mitch devotes at least an hour a morning to futzing around in his bathroom, the one he recently gutted because the toilet was the wrong color and, more importantly, according to him, faced the wrong way.

I want to tell him to go fuck himself; that I'm needy and not asking for much. Just some reciprocation for all the problems of *his* that I've patiently listened to. Returning calls once in a while. Maybe an invite to something paralleling all the meals I've cooked for him and his wife, the several U.S. Open tennis tournaments I've taken them to, the gardening I've taught and done for them around their starter house. But, highly attuned to my friendship-deficit, not wanting to lose this last pathetic one, I don't say what I want and, instead, actually consider accompanying him to get his hair colored, an idea I reject, securing instead a long-overdue invitation to an early Sunday dinner.

Sunday, when I arrive, the giveaway is the large bottle of vodka, almost empty, set in the remains of a melting block of ice in which it had been frozen, presumably by Mitch, who takes ceremonial culinary flourishes as seriously as he does the direction he faces taking a crap. The once-iced bottle now floats in a galvanized tub on the table on their rear deck.

To reach the deck, I pass through the living room where Mitch's father and mother-in-law are lying, their bodies draped over the sofa, their drunken mouths shaped like the tormented ovals in the faces in Picasso's *Guernica*. Out back, around the table and facing the Absolut shrine, I find Mitch's sober, irritated-looking wife, Rhona, plus Mitch passed out with his head splayed back. There's also Rhona's elderly father, who, as I near the table, awakens, shuddering like he's having a heart attack, then immediately pukes. My timing is good; I quickly repurpose an empty salad bowl, maneuvering it under his mouth, successfully catching his vomit.

"Hi, Rhona," I say, pausing to see which one of us will be the first to comment on this magical family moment.

"No one's cooking dinner," Rhona says, rolling her eyes and shrugging.

I already knew this; she doesn't cook, I'm not cooking and, really, no one seems that hungry.

I take this relatively private moment with Rhona to mention my burgeoning relationship with Francesca, who I'd introduced to Mitch and Rhona when Francesca and I first went out. Rhona tells me that she and Francesca now attend something called spin class together, and that she babysits for Francesca's two young kids.

"We can go out as couples!" Rhona exclaims, never missing an opportunity to anticipate a social event. "It'll be so fun!"

Francesca and I make dinner plans, ones that take some time arranging. It's our first get-together since she called out of the blue. There are the logistics of two young children on her end and my cousin just in from Florida complicating things on mine. I'm buoyed by the unabashed enthusiasm with which she works on our reunion. She emails me day to day on her efforts to enlist her nanny and, failing that, a neighborhood teenager to watch her kids.

After some nervous pleasantries, and a first bottle of wine that, true to form, I mostly consume, I'm imagining her straddling me in the backseat of my car, which, I must admit, I parked in the most secluded corner of the restaurant's lot. Her divorce is final. Her ex isn't meeting his financial obligations. She's struggling to maintain her large house. Her young kids are acting out. Save for the fact that we've already slept together, this could be just another first Match date with a divorcee.

But there's also a palpable enthusiasm that makes me feel like we're in a bubble where no one else in the restaurant exists or matters. I'm working towards convincing her that my divorce is on track as surely as the Coney Island roller coaster plummets. I'm debating whether to start with the fact that I've moved out or maybe explain the little that's left to decide in the mediation process the STBE and I have opted for.

"I met him at parenting class," I hear her say, the word *him* jolting me as I shift from offense to defense. The notion of a *him* wasn't something I expected, and if the *him* isn't her new nanny, then it kind of runs counter to all that a reasonable person in my position would infer from the longing-laced, explicit sexual banter that preceded this rendezvous.

"What?"

"His name is Bill. He's in advertising. I met him at parenting class. Would you believe, he lives on my block!"

"Parenting class?"

"You know. That Connecticut thing that parents with kids have to go to before getting divorced?"

"You met *him* there?"

"I hear lots of people, well, meet people there."

I'd been to *parenting class*. Two four-hour sessions that the law in Connecticut requires divorcing parents with minor children to attend. Eight hours of bitching by self-righteous hypocrites, and free *sharing* by sympathy-deserving people unable to get unhitched from some pretty horrible, ungrateful and/or self-centered partners.

The bejeweled, painted Darien, Connecticut filly complaining that her already twice-married STBE has been seduced by a much younger, conscienceless woman, which, based on my back-of-the-napkin calculation, is what she did to his first wife. The poor Irish guy trying to establish Connecticut residence, pouring his heart out about his wife refusing to give him a divorce in New York, where the law lets people string things out for decades. The Filipino lady who doesn't have the money to fight for her kids, or return home, imported by some rich Greenwich financial guy who threw their marriage under a train when he became bored. The white guy in his fourth year of living in the same house with an STBE to whom *soon* is geologic.

This Black Hole of Calcutta for awful relationships. This *Rashomon* for marital train wrecks. *This* is a notorious pick-up spot?

"Soup?" asks Maria, the restaurant's owner, soup being what I'm beginning to feel like I'm in.

"He's got four kids," Francesca says.

"Not very Jewish of him."

"Catholic. When I thought I was pregnant, which turned out to be wrong, but anyway, when I told him I was having an abortion, he went nuts. I couldn't believe it."

"So you're sleeping with a priest who's willing to ravish beautiful young Jewesses right on your own block? How convenient."

"Not exactly ravish . . ."

"Enough to think he got you pregnant," I say, fishing for what exactly *not exactly ravish* means.

"With six little kids between us, coordination is hairy."

"Just get them all on the same soccer team. Those games take a couple of hours," I say, hoping my suggestion sounds more sarcastic than constructive. "So if he gets you pregnant, you'll fight about an abortion."

"That's a problem."

"I can hear your mother screaming about the kid's christening."

"Won't happen," she says, looking down.

"He can support you?"

"I'm going back to being a physical therapist. Opening my own practice. I'm not interested in that."

What I really want to ask is *What are you interested in? Why are you here?* But I don't. I think maybe she's equivocal, having doubts about this guy, their relationship showing cracks into which I can insert wedges. I just need to give it time so I can decipher, make subtle moves, become useful, establish reliability, make amends whether warranted or not.

"I've thought about you a lot," I say, deciding to take her off the spot.

Her "me too" generates a warmth that carries me through dessert and an after-dinner Calvados, dissipating only when she says that Bill's agreed to her demand for couples therapy.

"But you're not even married."

"Better yet," she says. "Easier to take steps."

"But *couples therapy* to get rid of a religious conviction? Isn't that like gay deprogramming?"

"Maybe more issues," she says, elating me.

So I'm courting Francesca. I mean a full-court press. I run around meeting her for coffee, lunch, dinner. I re-pot her houseplants. Do work in her yard. Teach her kids to make pizza. Drive her to the city to meetings with a Texas relative who's bankrolling her new physical therapy practice. To help her with that enterprise, I introduce her to every chiropractor and orthopedist I know who'll send her clients in return for her sending them patients. And I find Hispanics who, for a fee, will recruit Central and South Americans from nearby immigrant communities. Supposedly injured and with health or workers' compensation insurance, they're potentially paying clients from sources that physical therapists haven't yet fully tapped.

But every time I try to touch, hold or kiss her, she pulls back.

"Texas sounds good," I say when Francesca invites me to join her at her bankrolling relative's house in Dallas.

"We'll have our own bedrooms," she volunteers.

"Then why would I go?" I ask.

"We're still doing the couples therapy," she says of the boyfriend. "I want to give it a little more time."

Couples therapy still? The writing's all over the wall. Big as pro-Castro graffiti in Havana. I'm having another go at a no-go. I'm doing the same old teenage thing of pursuing someone who's sending *cavalry's coming* smoke signals, maybe even *hit the bomb shelter, the nuke's on its way* urgent bulletins, actually *the reactor's in meltdown, get the hell out of here* dire warnings that she really isn't into me. I have to stop seeing her. Replace this yearning for her with something else, a powerful, countervailing addiction.

I try replacing Francesca with Match.com women. None work. Not the woman recounting her bondage episodes, nor the one who just successfully concluded her bedbug infestation. Not the one describing her visit to a sex aid store as timely because she just began masturbating.

I'm drinking and pill-popping and smoking pot, my deepest descent into booze and drugs since my teenage years and twenties. This moral slide is carried on between torrid, sexually explicit emails from Francesca that I put on hold as best I can when the kids are around, staying sober to cook for and eat with them, convincing myself that they're unaware of my down-going.

Though I think I'm being a proper parent when they're around, supervising and, I think, not being overly irritable or irrational, I do consider whether it'd be better for them to stay with their mother. But I keep them coming to me, not because I think I'm good for them, but because I'm afraid I'll lose their love. Their presence also happens to be about the only thing limiting my drinking.

Vowing not to answer Francesca's calls or read any more of her emails or do anything more for or with her, the very next night I'm dropping her off in the pouring rain after a movie. My pickup's cabin is steamy. My dog, once again having earned his nickname, Dogdini, by having opened her front door while we were out, is soaking wet from wandering around in the rain and emitting his wet-hair perfume from the back.

"So?"

"So Bill is promising to do anything I want," she says casually, like she's describing something she just read about some other couple in *People*. "Therapy. Whatever."

Bill again? Doesn't it bother her to invite my romancing while simultaneously patching things up with Bill? We all like having something to fall back on . . . professions, savings, less-crowded restaurants where reservations aren't necessary. But what of doing it with people? Thinking how I don't deserve this makes me realize that I'm begging the question, which is why am I putting up with this, taking the bait, letting myself be used, giving chase?

"And you find that—"

"Appealing?" she interrupts. "Kind of. Yeah. I don't know. It's confusing," she says, staring into my eyes like we're about to go at it, opening the car door to signify that we're not.

I watch her scurry up the stone steps to the house, getting soaked as she fumbles with her umbrella and the door. Seeing me watching, she runs back. Alcohol raises my hope for something that a tiny, sober corner of my brain knows only happens at the end of moronic melodramas, which, come to think of it, is exactly what this looks like. Inside the car, this beautiful drowned cat kisses me deeply, then more, then leaves. I desperately want the last of the Absolut, and for it to be both the last of it and of her, but I don't want to wash away the taste of her deep kiss, not just yet.

Once home, I ask my cousin for a Zantac, which, for the hundredth time since she's introduced me to the wonders of fast, anxiety-releasing drugs, she corrects me about, explaining that Zantac is for heartburn; Xanax is the anti-anxiety drug she's giving me. But isn't heartburn what I've got? None of this makes much sense to someone who's assiduously avoided drugs (except alcohol) since amphetamines, psychedelics and pot put me in a psychological hole that I had to dig myself out of in my twenties.

I pop the Xanax, then more vodka, risking drug and alcohol interactions for short-term relief.

I'm not worrying about interactions as I peruse my emails for something from Francesca. I table, but don't dispense with the idea of calling her. I decide first to troll Match for what came up in yesterday's nets but, just then, the phone rings. It's the broker selling the Ponderosa. Seems the Ponderosa, where the STBE remains ensconced, is filled with paint-slinging workers almost every time the broker shows it.

And then there's the fat pig ex-boyfriend of the STBE's sister, whom the STBE is paying two-fifty a day out of joint money to do odd jobs that, as far as I can see, consist exclusively of sleeping on the family room couch when prospective buyers come through. The broker says that yesterday the STBE had all the doorsills covered with flower petals, and had candles, incense and roses in vases put on all the counters and furniture tops. Something about *"feng shui-ing* bad vibes" out of the house. *Whose bad vibes could those be?*

The broker wants to know what to do. I consult my STBE pilot's log, my user manual compiled over decades navigating her shoals. It says fight for things that matter, like keeping the STBE from severing your relationship with your children. "Sorry," I tell the broker. "You're on your own."

My home-cooked squash soup, with just enough fried sage leaves and puréed leeks, does its trick on Francesca, getting me invited to chain-saw a tree that's fallen across her patio, all the while following her couples counseling reports that manipulate my hopes.

I'm looking at the sweat forming in the crack of Francesca's shorts that I see from my "down dog" yoga position behind her at the "something-ini" yoga center, an exercise barn that I follow her to on Wednesdays. Each week I wonder if I am the only one who notices that the furnace is still running though it's over ninety degrees inside.

I realize I have to stop being her lap dog.

"It is the heart, not appearances, that speaks to me," says the Peruvian beauty I meet on Match and hope diverts my attention. This said, I can't help noticing that this woman is done up to the nines in her Match photos, down to a tiny black cheek mole so perfect in size, shape and placement that it seems intentionally applied to contrast with and therefore draw attention to how otherwise perfect she looks. Determining that we have nothing in common except perhaps her tolerance for less attractive, shorter guys, I write to her with a mix of intellect and passion.

"Have you read any Mario Vargas Llosa?" I ask, referring to the well-known Peruvian author whose subjects I love, but whose baroque style I can't stand.

"How nice you know my country's literature," she writes back, precipitating a bout of correspondence culminating in lunch at a restaurant in the Village, a Peruvian one I pander to her with.

She arrives in front of the restaurant on Seventh Avenue near Sheridan Square. She's all that I imagined and more: a young Sônia Braga, light skin, dark eyes and hair, fulsomely feline. As we lay eyes on each other, our facial expressions demark the end-points on a spectrum of human emotion: my adulation, her horror. Trying to salvage something, I agree to share traditional appetizers and main courses consisting of barbequed bits of cow innards.

I know she's departing never to respond to or see me again. But my dick thinks—and its thinking is notoriously transaction-oriented—that it's still a good idea to continue pursuing her. So when it appears that she may miss the next bus to wherever she lives in New Jersey, I gallantly hail her a cab and inveigle the Haitian driver to drive like a maniac to the Port Authority Bus Terminal. There, I guide her like my life depends on it through escalators the likes of which I haven't seen since the Eiffel Tower, getting her on board her bus with just seconds to spare. I'm hoping that all this sweating and worrying and inveigling and running count for something which, per unanswered phone calls over the next few days, it apparently doesn't.

Day after day, similar experiences. A beautiful young Palestinian who enjoys my company but is troubled by our huge age disparity, a problem not bridged by my suggestion that she call me Grandpa. The attractive head of public relations for one of the big pharma companies. She's as pretty as she is humorless about her predatory work. The chemo-siren, a woman who spent most of lunch blaming aging hormones for the recent decline in the quality of her suitors.

"It was like I was emitting pheromones," she says between rather large nibbles on the turkey-brie-honey-mustard baguette she selected for lunch, describing her last time online, four years ago, before she met her recently dispatched boyfriend.

"I don't know what's changed," she says, presumably unhappy with those she's now attracting, present company apparently included; the problem, according to her, being now-missing pheromone emissions. She seems to be correct about this; the only essence I'm detecting is a hint of detachment from reality, coupled with the slight scent of marine life at low tide, the latter presumably reflecting her recently consumed luncheon brie.

I have to do something; this just isn't distracting me from Francesca.

STUCK IN THE PASSING LANE

A *New York Times* article by someone called a research anthropologist makes me think that maybe I have to make adjustments. This involves rebalancing what the author says are the "three independent systems" responsible for "human partnerships," namely "sexual attraction, romantic yearning and long-term attachment." These "very fickle" systems "can act together or they can act separately," which explains "why people can be wildly sexually attracted to those they have no romantic interest in, and romantically drawn to—or permanently attached to—people who hold no sexual interest."

I'm out with my third "long-term attachment" project, the third woman I've dated since learning that I have to pump steroids into my "long-term attachment" module, while desensitizing my "sexual attraction" and "romantic yearning" aspects. The prior two were fine people, each of whom I went out with twice; the first time to note that I had no interest, the second, what I call the BOD (Benefit of the Doubt) date, to confirm that all my wiring was intact during the first encounter, all readings correct, nothing overlooked.

The current choice my system's not going for is Marleen, her cuteness being distilled away by her rigidity, the personality equivalent of the hundreds of pounds of weights she lifts, and the long workouts she does every day, all to win the macabre female bodybuilding contests she trains for. Her body, probably flat and taut in all the wrong places, is something I'm desperately trying to prepare myself for seeing, to make myself "choose" to want to get into.

I assume that she keeps inviting me to her condo for that purpose, and by now I'm down to asking about the fiber makeup of the contents of her Pier 1 pillows and the countries of origin of her Ikea furniture, having run out of things to do there to avoid sitting quietly together, having already closely examined every photo, scrapbook and book (yearbooks and the scary *A Female Bodybuilder's Life* included), plus asked about every piece of artwork including, most recently, a crumpled orange-red piece of construction paper on a bookcase that, she informs, is garbage left by a kid, not sculpture.

It's a week before Thanksgiving, a holiday that used to be quite festive, with me a happy drunk cooking a notoriously good meal for the extended family. I don't have my kids this year, have no place to go except Marleen's, and don't want to be alone. So I'm desperately trying to hold on to whatever relationship I have with her until after the holiday.

The problem, though, is that almost every time I get near her, she edges closer; she wants physical contact. For my part, I'd rather tongue kiss the Michelin Man. To avoid real physical contact, and the conversation about my feelings or lack thereof that would prompt, I'm keeping us as busy as possible with physical activities, at least until Thanksgiving. We've slowly hiked every trail, some twice, in our relatively trail-less Connecticut suburb. We've ever so slowly plodded through every room in the two museums that exist in all of Fairfield County. We've laboriously perused every single *cute* antique store within thirty miles. But now, the day before the holiday, I'm cornered. I'm sitting idly with her on the sofa in her condo living room. I'm about to be smooched, no options left, nothing to do except let it happen and then discuss why it's not happening or, as I do, not wanting to discuss or explain, rising and leaving.

I WISH I HAD A PICTURE...

THANKSGIVING ARRIVES WORSE than I expected. Francesca's and Bill's families are spending it together, which I would have deemed psychologically wrong were I their couples therapist. Her email this morning is a glorious sexy recount of a day last year when we made out in Mianus River Park. Both of us were oblivious to a young child who, during one of our brief pauses for air, we noticed staring up at us.

My children are at a potluck dinner with the STBE's extensive family at the Ponderosa, the STBE, a non-cooker, probably contributing something out of her recently acquired self-help book *Over-Boiled and Burnt: Feeling Good, Cooking Bad*. As for me, I'm awake at dawn despite every fantasy I can concoct to keep me in bed, vodka and a bagel for breakfast, my cousin padding through the kitchen carrying her multi-chamber pill storage box in case I need something.

"What's the matter, honey?" she asks, like a motherly version of the babysitter she was when we were kids, me five years younger, her family living nearby.

Embarrassed by the pubescence of it, I haven't told her the story of Francesca, which I now relate, except for the email sexual intimacy.

"You need to find out what's really going on with her," she says, handing me a Xanax, then Absolut to wash it down. "Anyone you can call who knows her?"

Dialing Mitch, I realize that her advice, despite the meddling, is a welcome salve. My fear and pain diminish in the face of this modest suggestion that, judging from the relief I'm getting, feels like a multifaceted action plan devised by the Rand Corporation.

"Hey, it's Jed."

"How're you doing?" asks Mitch's wife, Rhona. During the day, he never answers the phone. Instead, she intercepts all potential interruptions that might interfere with his *thinking*, even, apparently, on Thanksgiving.

I ask if Mitch is in, though I know he is, because he almost always is, Rhona's screening often being tougher to penetrate than a Bombay call center's supervisory chain of command.

"I think he's on a conference call," she says, not offering to check, not the least bit self-conscious about using this excuse on Thanksgiving Day and for a guy who doesn't have anything to be *in conference* about. She's waiting for me to leave a message, give up, go away.

"Could you check?" I ask, knowing that he's probably just ensconced in his high-tech office surrounded by multiple bouncing ball screensavers and a battery of silent copying, scanning, faxing and other unidentifiable machines—everything he's put together for his nascent product development business.

"Well, I know he's *waiting* for a call," she says, like she's protecting her boss from the client from hell. "Oh, that soup was deee-lish," she says, referring to the roasted squash soup I left on their doorstep a few days ago.

"I just need to ask him something."

"I can have him—"

"Rhona," I interrupt. "I'm returning his call," I say, daring her to suggest I'm lying, which we both know is true, forcing her to choose between insulting me and derailing Einstein's train of thought. She elects destroying the master's concentration. Mitch agrees to meet me in an hour.

The waterfall, eye level outside the windows of the basement bar of Cobb's Mill Inn, is wonderful; ducks, outside, oblivious to the descending water, lined up on the ledge, the water's point of no return. And the scene is even better today, Thanksgiving Day, because Mitch and I find the bar empty of people and yet open.

Coming down the winding Colonial-era stairs, I see Mitch already is there, already working through a martini. I sit, my martini arrives and, as I'm dispatching it, I get through the beginning of the story about Francesca.

"So what's going on now?" he asks, interrupting when I pause for a breath, apparently tiring of details that don't involve him.

I speed up, getting quickly to Francesca and I recently reacquainting, our dinner that I had such high hopes for that were sunk by her revealing she's got this boyfriend Bill. Pausing, looking up, I see that Mitch is watching the ducks, probably wondering what they're thinking of him. Heading towards the Francesca-rainy-kiss thing, I make the mistake of sucking in a small bit of air that I need to keep telling the story and not suffocate. Mitch, ever vigilant for conversation-turning moments, interrupts, refocusing things on himself.

"I guess I could have fucked her," he says, nonchalantly returning to sipping his drink. "She liked me. A lot."

"What?"

"We've been out a few times with them. I definitely could have fucked her if I wanted," Mitch repeats.

I'm struggling not to use some Israeli military move on him, perhaps a single, stiff-armed assault driving his martini glass through his mouth and into his brain. At the same time, I'm barely holding my tongue as I'm on the brink of saying, *Mitch, she's a beautiful, refined, well-educated woman with sophisticated European sensibilities.*

She'd be about as likely to want you to fuck her as Juliette Binoche would want to get it on with Sylvester Stallone.

"She's always breaking up with Bill," Mitch says, interrupting the flow of my unspoken tirade.

"What?"

"Yeah. Always fighting with the boyfriend. Breaking up. She bitches. He apologizes. They get back together. They've been breaking up as long as we've known them."

I'm feeling like I'm what real estate brokers call a *stalking horse*: a bidder the seller uses to get the buyer she really wants to up his offer. I'm being used to drive Bill-the-boyfriend to make even bigger concessions, like maybe converting to her religion. *A bad deal*, I think, imagining this good Catholic with a few bad ideas transformed into a rabidly kosher, Sabbath-observing, all-the-time praying, Israel-is-always-right Jew. But, realistically, the woman obviously needs security. A retired old wolf like me, one seemingly making up for lost time, doesn't stand a chance against a solid, young, down-the-block advertising executive with four little kids that nest with hers like toy Russian dolls.

I don't know what I was thinking when I went after her again, but I know what I'm feeling now, which is fixated on something I know for sure I'll never get. I tell myself she's just another person, nothing special, that I'll find someone else, that I probably don't even care for her personally, that it's just the not getting that's motivating me, like Jay Gatsby pining for Daisy Buchanan in *The*

Great Gatsby. But I can't help feeling empty, worthless, lost. This thinking douses my oil fire of bad feelings with water, spreading them wider, deeper.

At home, the envelope on the counter contains a few Xanax and my cousin's note saying, consistent with her nonstop rescuing of people not in need, that she's temporarily decamped for the STBE's house, not wanting to leave the STBE alone as the children are coming to me tomorrow for a highly unpopular, newly created holiday: Second Thanksgiving with Dad. I pop some Xanax, pour some Absolut over ice and go on Match to see who's looking on Thanksgiving: Come all ye boozed-up, lonely people like me.

I've seen the introductory phrase this woman uses in her profile. It's the qualifier, "My friends say that I am." It's her way of implying that what follows is a Pew Research-vetted opinion rather than her own hubristic claim. *At least,* I think, *she's making an effort not to sound full of herself.* And then there are her personal characteristics, sort of an ad agency-invented laundry list of features designed to attract a wide audience: goes to the theatre and movies; stays in for quiet nights snuggling; laughs often; likes serious conversation; exercises regularly. She eats well, often at *destination* restaurants, but also appreciates small local places, the ones, I assume, where the decibel level is sufficiently low that lip-reading isn't a prerequisite for the serious talk she likes. She's confident and take-charge, but also "vulnerable" and able "to go with the flow."

And, though she lives in New Jersey, she does satisfy many of the other requirements on my evolving and increasingly superficial shopping list: under fifty; divorced (not separated); a non-memoir-length profile with proper capitalization and devoid of text-message abbreviations; has children who neither are infants nor described as some supernatural power's most sublime gift. What I also appreciate is that her photos are of her only, meaning no dogs, flowers, beaches or children, nor any with encircling arms whose associated bodies and faces have been Photoshopped out. And she'll meet today. Toasting my good fortune, I swig some Absolut.

I'm making a wide, inebriated swing with my pickup into the parking lot of the restaurant she's picked. This lands me squarely in line for its mandatory valet parking, an ominous sign that I've again made a duo of greenhorn dating mistakes, the first being letting myself be euchred into anything but coffee at Starbucks, and the second being letting the woman pick the place.

The valet opens my door before I finish gathering myself up enough so, hopefully, I don't have to brace an arm against the car to avoid falling. This, I'm thinking, isn't good. Not driving drunk used to be a rule—and still is when I'm with my kids. But when alone I let the rule slip, as if it's my unique, inalienable right to kill myself, a liquor-truncated logic ignoring everyone else I could take with me.

The place is a steakhouse, one encased with enough mahogany to make caskets for the entire Mormon Tabernacle Choir. My nose presses against the paneling, a very robust, swirly Bohemian grain. The cows slaughtered for this restaurant, though, are not being fed grain, as evidenced by the fifty-a-plate "corn-fed" cuts of beef on the "specials" board by the *maître d*'s stand, a blackboard written on by someone with excellent penmanship that isn't meant to be read on one's knees, judging from the arm I'm feeling gently but firmly lifting me.

I struggle to look steady. I scan the bar, which is filled with lots of grandparents and children. I remember it's Thanksgiving Day. These are the extended families that want to strictly limit their time together, just order, eat and, blessedly, leave. I don't see any unattached women, so I move closer where I see a tiny hand waving vigorously in my direction that I'm hoping isn't waving at me.

The hand belongs to a woman who looks like a child. I don't mean adolescent or Lolita-like. I mean, if she's four foot six, I'm Shaq. She's smiling, saying hello, offering her lips for a kiss, which I give, me hoping people see that she's wearing lipstick, eye shadow, and a very small, probably extensively hemmed strapless black evening dress with heels. The sum of all this I hope eliminates any thoughts harbored by those around us that I'm a pedophile.

We're seated thankfully near a waiter who furnishes a wine list. I immediately order the first red I see.

I mentally run through a list of nervous opening questions, trying to select one unlikely to generate an unpleasant response. Hard as it is to believe, this type of immensely unpleasant experience could get worse, and has in the past. For example, sometimes when I ask, "What do you do?" I get, "It's in my profile. I guess you only looked at the pictures." Or when I ask, "How old are your children?" I get, "Don't have any. You must be confusing me with some *other* woman."

"So how long have you been divorced?" I ask, sitting back, pouring myself more wine, hoping she'll launch into a divorce saga that, with a few digressions produced by some gently interruptive interrogatories, could take us clear through the main course.

"That's the thing," she says, stopping.

The thing? I think to myself. *What thing?*

"It's tough, huh?" I ask, struggling to pay attention, hoping to kick-start a long oration in which she's so absorbed that my zoning out isn't noticed.

"Yeah," she says, her explanation stalling, the focus now back on me, where I absolutely don't want it to be.

I'm thinking that her story needs some impetus, some strong motivation propelling it forward. I'm hoping to find the inspiration for that in the next bottle that I'm ordering. Happily, I notice that she isn't drinking much of *my* wine.

"So," I say, pausing. On the advice of the wine, incautiously I proceed, asking if her ex sees their children, hoping they have some.

"Just about every day. You see, he's still in the house," she says, sighing as if resigned to the fact that, given enough time, I'll stumble upon a question she can't answer in two words.

"Didn't the divorce end that?" I ask, now slipping on loose rock on a steepening slope.

"Well, we're not divorced yet," she says, explaining, a few hundred questions and another bottle later, that her still *husband*, who *doesn't* want the divorce, is a New Jersey judge. But not just any New Jersey judge; he's the judge presiding over the courthouse where her divorce is pending, which, from being a lawyer, I know is legal as long as he isn't hearing her specific case. As a lawyer, I also know that the *presiding* judge is the one who controls just about everything every other judge in that courthouse really cares about—mainly their parking spaces. In that capacity, he can, if he wants, by threatening to revoke parking privileges, get the judge who is hearing her case to extend it beyond her life expectancy.

"Are you ready to order, sir?" the waiter asks, interrupting this very unpleasant interlude. But I'm not ready to order and don't anticipate that status changing anytime soon. So, drawing on my growing wealth of dating experience, and justifying myself on the ground that I've been misled, I get up, drop enough cash on the table to cover the couple of bottles of wine I've mainly had and, as politely as I can, excuse myself.

The teenage valet lurches my pickup into the restaurant driveway, driver's ed apparently no longer covering manual transmissions. The car behind me toots because I'm not moving, which I'm not doing until I lower all the windows with the hand cranks. The valets probably wonder, *Why in November?* I'm hoping that the cold wind on my face will keep me awake and get me home in one piece. Also, where I can, I'm taking the big federal roads, the New Jersey Turnpike, the Cross-Westchester Expressway, the Connecticut Turnpike, their ample widths and shoulders providing a safety net for staying on the road, sort of like ordering shots in big martini glasses, their wide brims ensuring I won't miss my mouth at the end of a long night of drinking.

Having finished off what's left of the pint in the glove compartment, realizing I'm hungry, I'm pulling off the Connecticut Turnpike into the last rest stop before my exit, McDonald's cheeseburgers and fries sounding good. I'm following an eighteen-wheeler that stops just past the turnoff for the take-out window, which, I realize, we've both missed. Hemmed by a car behind me, I'm figuring I'll have to go around and come back. I'm waiting for the eighteen-wheeler to get going when I realize that the back corner of the truck's coming directly at me, straight at my windshield. For an instant I deny it, then accept that he's about to cleave me, which won't change because he can't see me in his mirrors, and my horn, which I'm pounding, isn't getting a response.

I try opening my door but it's blocked by a dumpster inches away. There's not enough time to jump the stick and escape the passenger side, the corner of his truck now practically on me. There isn't a backseat door to escape through, and the car behind isn't helping. So I slam the wheel left, hit the gas and run the pickup into the dumpster which, though taking a big long chunk out of my pickup, moves the dumpster and yields enough space for me to squeeze by and jump the median which lands me in front of a take-out order machine blabbing, "Your order please." To my surprise, I hear myself order, only to throw up at the window where they ask for money and give the food.

I find the truck's driver in the parking lot and explain what happened. He mutters something about me being in the wrong lane, then gets out a camera that, from his nonchalance, must be standard equipment, like CB radios and dirty magazines. Obviously, accidents like this are routine, the guy taking photos of everything, including my driver's side that looks like it's been keyed with a pickaxe.

I'm thinking that I wish I had a picture of me. Not of me right now, crying. Of me in my other life, when I had purpose: one hundred and fifty employees, four offices and a half million in monthly payroll. Acres of gardens that appeared in magazines and won awards. All before the woman I took good care of for twenty-plus years started running around trying to make me look dishonest and disloyal and mean and dysfunctional to my children. Now, I'm just another nonworking boozehound.

I'm crying so hard that the truck driver steps back, apparently afraid I'm about to do something unpredictable, maybe crazy. He'd just moved forward, all twitchy and in my face, because I wasn't agreeing to sign something absolving him. Now he's scared, probably because I look like I don't give a shit, which is true. My life has stopped mattering.

HOUSTON, WE HAVE A PROBLEM

I'M ON THE BEDROOM FLOOR clinging to my mutt like a plank in the open ocean. For a couple of days, just about all I've been able to do is walk and feed him.

I know that I'm in a place that's unsafe because there are no rules, structures, goals. I don't care about anything, not even brushing my teeth. There aren't any people around—no customers, employees, children, women—so pleasing people isn't something that keeps me busy. I've got no interest in reading, seeing movies, starting businesses, cooking, gardening, taking care of my kids. I could care less about the just-stolen presidential election, the Iraq War, Israel's treatment of the Palestinians, events that previously would have seriously concerned me. I might just as well be comatose in a hospital bed, my living will being very specific about what's to happen to me in this circumstance.

What brought me here is seeing all roads leading nowhere. Nothing has worked out, despite intense effort. Without any needs or desires or goals, I have no reason to be sober, ever. So I don't need to play the games that I used to that kept me from being a nonstop drunk. The rule of always being sober at work. The rule of not drinking until the kids are in bed. The rule of finishing all my paperwork before grabbing the Absolut. The test of periodically not drinking for a day or a week to suggest the false truth that I can stop pickling my liver whenever I want.

I've got my little personal phonebook in one hand, and I'm using my thumb to push past pages. I'm looking for the phone number of a guy who once looked with what seemed like dread at each drink that I ordered. He is, like me, the father of a child with type 1 diabetes, and I reached out to him once when this disease struck one of my kids. Now I'm looking for a different kind of help.

"Pat?"

"Yes."

"It's Jed. Helena's dad."

"How are you? Everything okay with Helena?"

"Yeah, best as can be expected."

"What's up?"

"Can you help me?"

"Are you okay for the night?"

"Yes."

"I'm up in Maine, but some of my buddies will meet you tomorrow morning at eight at the diner on Putnam. Know where that is?"

"Yes."

"They'll know who you are. Just get there."

"Okay."

"And if things get worse tonight, call me. Don't worry about the time."

Driving to the diner, I'm thinking how strange it is that he knew why I was calling without me explaining a thing. Or did he? Maybe I'm heading to the local evangelical cabal, the help I'm about to receive being a heavy dose of robotic spiritualism. I don't know, and when I slide into the booth with the guys who motion towards me, I still don't know. And when they ask if I'd been to AA before, the term means nothing to me.

"Where's Master?" one of the guys asks.

"Master's always late," the guy across says. "Let's order."

I'm not hungry but, not wanting to stick out, I order what they order, a lot of eggs and bacon and toast and gallons of coffee. The waitress brings it quickly, seemingly knowing their need. My food just sits as I listen to idle conversation about bicycles and kids and who went to which meeting that I'm parsing for something suggesting what I'm getting into. Their main topic is Master's whereabouts, which makes me so wary that I watch the door every time it opens looking for a guy with a

Jonestown-Guyana tan lugging a plastic jug of Kool-Aid. Then Master arrives, a big, chubby guy in bicycle-riding spandex. He slides in across from me and is greeted by the others without any genuflecting or ring kissing.

With Master in tow, we move on to a meeting down the road. I follow their cars and, when we arrive, I worry even more because the meeting is in the back of a church in a room packed with excessively cheerful men, me sitting way in the back with Master next to me like he's keeping an eye on the new recruit. From his nearby perch, I assume Master notices my baffled stare during repetitive invocations of higher powers and gods and wills and powerlessness. I wait for him to elbow me when I don't raise my hand at the request of the guy up front who asks new people to identify themselves. Then they're holding hands in a circle saying a short prayer. After a total of about an hour, it's over.

Outside, I'm surrounded by welcoming men papering me with their phone numbers, making me feel like a prayer niche in the Wailing Wall, *everyone* telling me I'll feel better if I just don't drink and if I go to meetings. I cry because they care, which is strange since, from the stories I just heard, they're mainly ex-gutter drunks who've left a lot of wreckage in their wakes, people whose *caring* shouldn't mean much to the sophisticated, successful, carefully controlled drunk I think I am. Though my mind's working hard to devalue the comfort I'm receiving, my emotions rebel, pouring out tears, accepting their concern. These people, I realize, are giving me the gift of a place where I feel safe admitting I'm a drunk.

Someone gives me a directory of nearby meetings that makes my locale, Fairfield County, Connecticut, look like AA ground zero, there being meetings in almost every church basement, plus an entire AA-dedicated building.

I read the AA books—and there are a lot of them—and begin picking up advice that must have been edited out of my copy of life's user manual. I realize that I drink like most everyone else, to anesthetize feelings, in my case many things, including unfounded shame and self-induced resentment. The resentment thing, according to another bit of very illustrative AA lore, "is a poison you take expecting the other person to die." And though the guys are way too clubby for me, I decide that, at worst, it's a club and not a cult, which is confirmed when it turns out that *Master*, whose sole executive action is leading the race to the cookie jar during mid-meeting breaks, actually is *Tim Master*, just one of the guys.

For the time being, AA's the center of my life. The time I would otherwise spend drinking, or doing things that would make me want to drink, I now spend setting up chairs and making coffee for meetings, listening to other drunks, sometimes three times a day. The urge to drink recedes for the time being, except in restaurants where not ordering wine makes me feel people think I'm a child. Caring too much what other people think is just one of my problems.

Now I have to pick a *sponsor*, someone with years of sobriety whom I can call any time about anything, sort of a kind Judge Judy crossed with an alcoholic-focused Dr. Phil. I'm at the Tuesday morning meeting that I've made my *home group*, something no one's defined. I'm looking around the table for a sponsor. There's the guy who stays sober by "doing the right thing," usually something involving cleaning up after himself, like putting his used gum in the garbage or not leaving crap for his wife to throw out. Then, the regular who's always fighting with his wife, but not so loudly anymore, sobriety seemingly keeping the decibel level down. There's the guy who's switched professions from stockbroker to addiction counselor, giving advice perhaps part of the process of learning to take it. Then the broker, a devout Irish Catholic whose weekly sharing is infused with pain and shame, a public confession, his struggle with alcohol apparently his cross to bear. I shouldn't leave out Katherine, a fortyish, exuberant woman who gives me big hugs and joined AA at sixteen. Selecting her would give me access to immense "sobriety" as AA measures it, which is in years. But it would violate the unwritten same-sex sponsorship rule.

And then there's Ari.

After politely constraining himself while others speak, at an appropriately deferential point in the sharing process, Ari always raises his hand, launching into a well-paced, eloquent explanation of the sick, twisted things he's thought and, to an extent, resisted doing the past week, a well-orchestrated soliloquy that sounds extemporaneous but, I'm guessing, isn't. His very entertaining output demonstrates great intelligence (he's a patent attorney), and fast footwork (at one point he was both a raving drunk *and* an advisor to the U.S. Patent and Trademark Office). Ari reminds me of Russell Crowe in *A Beautiful Mind*, handsome, deeply thoughtful, unfairly troubled. On the theory that a scant milligram of whatever's keeping him sober should tame my alcoholism faster than penicillin cures clap, I pick him as my sponsor.

Though Ari has a busy consultancy practice, and travels a lot, he picks up almost every time I call, sometimes before the ring, making Ari seem, well, a bit psychic. And his consultative technique, invariably involving telling me about his experiences rather than what to do about mine, almost always refers to past encounters with his many ex-wives and enough drunken escapades to force the cops to digitize their *Ari* file.

"Ari? Is this an okay time?"

"Perfect. I'm driving to a meeting in Baltimore."

"My youngest daughter. I'm afraid I'm losing her. She won't switch houses anymore. Every discussion with her turns into yelling. I keep begging her mother not to interfere. To help me get some time with her. The kid doesn't want to spend time with me, is always accusing me..."

"You know your best thinking's what got you here," Ari says. That's AA-speak for "Forget about it," "Give it a rest," "Don't drive yourself crazy (and to drink)," "Try being quiet and non-willful for once in your life," and "Though you won't be able to take credit for doing something, you may well be pleasantly surprised at the outcome."

I've heard these admonishments a hundred times in our circles of trust and candor.

"What?" I ask, wanting to hear him say this again, reinforcing it.

"In my experience, when I have something going on that I'm thinking about a lot, this is what I tell myself," Ari says. "Like now, I'm about to sue my best client. Fuckers haven't paid my bill for six months. I'm definitely going to sue them."

"Really, Ari?" I ask, wondering whether he's giving me an example of something he's resisting acting on or, as it seems, asking me for advice. If I decide it's the latter, and I'm wrong, I risk perhaps violating some AA stricture about disciples knowing their places.

"When you sue them," I say, "you probably won't get more work from them." Being on the phone, unable to gauge his body language, I add, protectively, "Right?"

"I'm suing them. I've had it."

Emboldened by Ari listening, conversing, seemingly considering my thoughts, definitely not just shutting me down, I add the killer line: "You know your best thinking's what got you here, Ari."

I hear Ari's chuckle as he hangs up.

And so it goes, week after week, Ari and I getting advice by giving it, the nub essentially being don't give a shit about anything except not drinking, an approach to sobriety covered in any one of the many Alcoholics Anonymous treatises like *The Big Book*, or in some other very pithy compendium of AA thoughts, or perhaps in oral lore passed from drunk to drunk.

I'm told I shouldn't have a relationship for a year, which makes me want to resign, but I can't figure out who to give my resignation to and, anyway, I'll just ignore this admonition, something relatively minor in comparison with the killer one I do follow: *Don't drink.* I even change my Match profile to "Never Drink," a switch that generates lots of questions that indiscreetly seek to elicit whether I'm a drunk, questions I consider answering with "I'm allergic" before deciding on admitting I'm in AA.

I see a profile of a very cute girl who lives nearby. Her photos look like they were torn out of the Smirnoff Family Adventure Album: her hoisting martinis essentially everywhere, at parties, on motorboats, at basketball games, in restaurants, on beaches, skiing, in the backseats of cars. When she emails back that she likes me, but couldn't date someone who doesn't drink, clearly a most realistic assessment, I start drafting my "Okay, but let's have dinner anyway" email while, at the same time, reluctantly, getting a reality check from Ari.

"Jed. Good to hear from you. I'm on my way to pick up my kid at school to go look at a car."

"Getting rid of the BMW?"

"No, for him."

"What happened to his old one?"

"He trashed it. But he wants a motorcycle, and I told him he's absolutely not getting one."

"Really?"

"Well."

"Anyway," I say, "I kind of met someone who I'm thinking of going out with. But she drinks. Quite a bit I think. Honestly, her photos, the social things she describes, all seem to involve drinking."

"People, places, things," Ari says in enigmatic AA-speak. I've come to learn that this oft-used linguistic triptych is a solemn warning that what you do or don't surround yourself with affects whether you drink.

"Yeah, but I love not drinking," I say, pausing, realizing that I'm not even convincing myself that it's anything other than a very bad idea to go anywhere near this seemingly liquor-dependent woman. "Actually, I'm kind of uneasy about dating now that I'm not drinking,"

I continue. "I'm afraid I'm going to feel like I've got a problem that I'll be explaining every time someone orders drinks which, with this woman, could be every time the waiter passes by."

"I need to get an apartment in the city. What do you think that'll run?" Ari asks.

"Why?"

"I can't stay at home. Cleo's driving me crazy." Ari sounds more edgy than usual, less controlled, like his containment vessel's about to crack, his reference to Cleo being to his third and current wife, the one whose reign, I believe, marks the beginning of what an Ari psycho-historian would call his Age of Sobriety. I'm also noticing that Ari's advisory method isn't just to share a similar experience, like a time in the past when he also teased himself, as I am now, with a sobriety-threatening act. He's more selective. He shares present imminent threats in the form of swords hanging over his head. These real-time events, though far more riveting than history, also are confusing. Every time he does this, I feel like I'm taking my doubts about being kosher to a rabbi who's salivating over a pork sandwich.

"What are you gonna to do in the city, Ari?" I ask, hoping to telegraph that moving out from under his wife Cleo's surveillance doesn't seem like a sober "people, places, things" thing to do. Asking Ari this question makes me think that maybe Ari's strategy is to make me feel like Socrates, his way of teaching me to ask myself the important questions. Waiting like David Carradine for Ari to chuckle and perhaps affectionately call me "grasshopper" before signing off, I hear him hang up.

He's right, I think, as I craft another sucking up email to Ms. Constant Drinker who has since sent another. Hers I would subtitle "Booze Is My Co-Pilot," the email describing alcohol as the tie that binds her life together: golfing then drinking, sailing then drinking, getting off work then drinking, drinking then drinking. My email says that's okay and, showing my sense of humor, that I could be her permanent designated driver and, anyway, I say, like the TV-addicted Peter Sellers character in *Being There*, speaking at cross purposes with a prostitute who's asking what he wants: "I like to watch." As if gagged by some meddlesome extraterrestrial force, perhaps a "higher power" that's protecting me, to my great disappointment, she doesn't respond.

I'm sitting in the Tuesday morning meeting, planning the words I hope to get myself to speak, trying to sound brilliant like Ari and heartfelt like Katherine, telling myself that I shouldn't plan anything. I should just raise my hand with a blank mind like everyone else seems to do, which I try doing but doesn't work because the insecure, fearful people-pleaser in me won't let me turn the teleprompter off.

"I don't speak much," I say, setting the stage, drawing them in. "But I raised my hand today because I want to thank you all. I do listen. And what you've shared with me has helped me immensely in living my life. So many of the things that frustrated me, made me want to drink, though still there, frustrate me less. That's because you've taught me how wrong it is, no matter how right or needy I am, to expect things of people, to try to control what I can't, to fear losing what I'll never be able to convince myself I actually have." I have to pause for a moment to corral my emotions.

"Today's a pretty big day for me. My divorce became final and, after court, in the hall, my now ex-wife came over and said 'Thank you' to me. It's the first time I can remember her thanking me for anything in twenty-plus years, and though I had no idea what she was thanking me for, what I most noticed was that her thanks made me feel nothing. *Nothing.* The approval I'd sought and worked for from her for all these years, the relief from shame, I didn't want anymore. At least not from her, though I suspect I'll find another victim to shower with my endless bounty of helpfulness and, ultimately, when they're totally spoiled and taking advantage right and left, make the object of my resentments."

People laugh. I pause, regrouping for the denouement, which I'm nervous about because I'm considering going extemporaneous, which I do.

"So I'm facing a choice. I've learned to quiet myself. To be still. To keep inside the feelings that, when put into words, get me into trouble. But I know that a further step is necessary. I now have to find a way to forgive the women in my life, my mother and her facsimile, my now ex-wife because, selfishly speaking, that's the only way I'll be done with them and the feelings that make me want to drink. But every time I try on the feeling of forgiveness, I'm inundated with reruns of them chastising and berating and demanding and condemning me. The question, though, is whether I want to continue to suffer. I don't, and I don't deserve it."

How strange, I think, to be embarrassed by all the hugs I get afterwards. In the parking lot I see Ari pulling out in his Roadster. He waves, but otherwise ignores me, probably averse to complimenting a fellow people-pleaser. I know I should flag him down and clear what I'm about to do—take my first sober spin on the dating dance floor—but I don't.

Preparing, first I repackage myself on Match, offsetting the dating negative of "never drinks" by flipping my Match marital status from undesirable "separated" to highly valued "divorced." To properly portray myself, I make an appointment for next week to get photographed professionally, leaving this week to deal with my long-term problem—my receding hairline—first with a plastic surgeon who does hair transplants, and then with the Hair Club for Men, which says that what they do doesn't involve blood.

The ambiance of Dr. David Kirstein's full top-floor "Plastic and Reconstructive Surgery" suite magically combines the light, airy tranquility of a day spa with the dead seriousness of a funeral home. This, I'm sure, is the environment that various consultants have recommended for convincing people to fork over tens of thousands of dollars for what, at least initially per the magazines in the waiting room, makes your head look like a cornfield planted during a seed shortage. It's making me feel like I'm about to get a manipulative sales pitch, my suspicions heightening when someone gives me Dr. Kirstein's *before and after* photo book in which the photos don't show much difference to me.

Though I expect Dr. Kirstein's eyes to go where I don't want women's to go, to my deeply inverted hairline, he, instead, is examining my face, turning it from side to side, then sweeping around to take in my profile like I'm going to be drawn.

"Have you considered adjusting this?" he asks from behind me while pulling the skin on the sides of my eyes back.

"Adjust what?" I ask.

"Here," he says, releasing my skin, then pointing to sacks under my eyes that I hadn't really noticed and apparently he thinks should, shall we say, be lifted.

Dr. Kirstein goes on to explain, unsolicited, the utter simplicity and self-image benefits of blepharoplasty, which is eliminating lower eyelid bags, plus, for those of us not cheeky enough, cheek augmentation, plus some chin implants, plus some liposuction that involves cutting and filling my face like I'd once done to a hillside to make room for a pool. Realizing for the first time that plastic surgery offers those with money the opportunity to look like anyone they're not, I ask if he can make me Dustin Hoffman. I laugh. He doesn't. I leave.

My Hair Club for Men appointment is in a nondescript office building. I take the elevator to the ninth floor and, as instructed, walk directly across the hallway through a door marked only "Entrance." This must be for Hair Club members who want anonymity. *How bad could it be to have your cover blown?*

The intrigue continues in the waiting room, where everyone keeps his head down in a magazine, the impression being what I imagine a sperm bank waiting room feels like, so much so that I don't even want to touch the magazines.

"Tim, they're ready for you," the receptionist says, calling the next appointment. It is hard to see her since she's surrounded by hundreds of bottles of hair care products for sale.

Out of the corner of my eye, I watch Tim re-rack his *Sports Illustrated*. I also catch the guy next to me following

Tim as, for that matter, are all the guys I can see, all in the same way, heads down, eyes looking up, like we're faking prayer. And as Tim reaches the inner-sanctum door, with no possibility that he'll see us, we lift our heads in unison, like a troupe of voyeuristic Rockettes, riveting our eyes on Tim or, more specifically, the moon patch on the back of his head that we're all examining.

My new, all-natural, glued down, regularly serviced Hair Club for Men toupee now fitting as snugly as a condom, I replace my old Match photos with studio shots with my new hairdo. Going back on Match after this hiatus, I feel like a farmer returning to a field he's left fallow. Nothing much has changed, though; as before, the profiles mainly start with the phrase "I can't believe I'm doing this," as if decades of relationship failure isn't enough of a reason.

I opt for the Match function that displays the maximum number of women and minimum amount of text about each on a screen, then wait for my gonad-driven selection process to kick in. But it doesn't, at least not right away. The delay's making me uncomfortable, nervous, like I'm suffering from some new psychological disease, maybe Dating Dysfunction Disorder.

Instead of just honing in on photos, I find myself asking questions I can't answer, like does it matter that she's divorced or never been married, the never married perhaps having had a twenty-year out-of-wedlock relationship; the divorcee perhaps married only long enough to process the papers. And children versus none? She might have raised them with all the attention that sea turtles give the eggs they leave behind on beaches.

Does it mean anything that we both like "Water Sports"? "Tennis"? "Bingo"? And what if she's selected 118 out of Match's 120 of the world's most popular couples' activities, but omitted my favorites, gardening and simultaneous masturbation? And of those who have "a great family, good friends, and an entirely full life that's just missing one thing," what if the missing "thing" is a replacement for her worn-out dildo? And what are the chances that a woman with a "deep capacity for love, laughter, fun and intimacy," in reality, is insatiably and intolerably needy? And what could it possibly mean to be "sophisticated inside and out," especially inside?

And so like Columbus after his first landfall in the Bahamas—re-provisioned, enthusiastic, hopeful, yet unsure—I embark, reading and emailing and following up. I try to give the benefit of the doubt, struggling not to think that people are the opposite of what they say, that anyone listing an astrological sign is *ipso facto* ridiculous, that having things in common, such as enjoying walking, doesn't mean a fucking thing.

My first few dates are like slow descents, possibly not even qualifying as dates. I drive into the city to meet a woman who doesn't show up. Later, she says it's my fault that I didn't "call to confirm," something "everyone knows you have to do." She hangs up when I remind her that she never asked me to. Another woman, possibly her dating-challenged twin, makes plans, calls them tentative, requires that I call multiple times to see if her busy schedule has opened up, NASA shuttle launches being easier to schedule. And after a very long forty-five-minute lunch with a woman I can't wait to leave, while saying goodbyes on the street, my saying something polite but untrue, like "I'll call you," triggers tears and hysteria, something about us "getting along so well" and now her feeling "pushed away."

I try not to get down about these exceedingly poor initial results, deciding to try women more sensitive about others or at least less so about themselves, and trying to present a more empathetic, less sardonic me. I pick a fifty-five-year-old shrink, thinking shrinks may be especially sympathetic. She arrives at the restaurant with her wild hair filled with colorful chopsticks, a creative way to carry her eating utensils. She spends the evening explaining the psychological underpinnings of her pending divorce from her thirty-two-year-old husband of ten years, me thinking, though resisting saying, that it sounds more like disowning than divorcing.

The dates just get better and better. A social worker, another helper of others, bursts into tears about her breast cancer lump removed ten years earlier. Then a human resources director undergoes a werewolf-like facial change when I ask about her family. The question unleashes a tale of anger and abuse at the hands of a father and two older siblings. With my capacity for empathy at what I think is its lowest, an elementary school teacher digs a new bottom. She describes in DePalmaesque detail her STBE's third, at-home, bloody failed suicide attempt, the woman now apparently well aware of the need to maintain hefty stocks of paper towels.

I'm walking in New York's Theatre District, having just finished pre-theatre lunch with Marcy, who does something with stocks. We're heading for a Sunday matinee of *The Wiz*, a show she wants to see that I'm sure will nauseate me. We're getting along okay, by which I mean we're both doing each other the immense favor of not providing too much information too soon, a relief, I think, from all the woeful stories I've recently had to act like I care about.

The theatre is packed. Marcy goes to the restroom while I wait in the lobby, where, turning, amidst hundreds of people, I'm shocked to find myself directly across from my now ex-wife and my mother, the most distasteful of dynamic duos for me—the two having been enemies until the divorce provided a reason for them to become friends. And they see me. The ex stays in place but my mother, true to form, trots right over, just as Marcy gets back.

"Oh, Jed. Where are your seats?"

"Orchestra, Mom," I say, figuring the next shoe to drop is that we're sitting together. "Oh, and this is Marcy," I whimper as my mother gives Marcy the eyeball, her way of insisting on being introduced.

"We're in the balcony. We'll lean over and spit on you," Mother says, laughing, this, to her, apparently a joke. But where is the humor in the karmic implication of this chance meeting? Plus, Marcy smokes, which I can't stand, straining this relationship, initiating a dribbly end of blasé phone calls and busy-already invites.

I must, I think, find another way.

Again, I decide I must be making mistakes. I'll expand my search field. But I'm already what I'd call very much an equal-opportunity dater, someone who allows all manners of women to not infatuate and disappoint him: ethnicities; occupations; educational backgrounds; marital, parental and immigration statuses; ages; even women whom I don't find attractive because of the way they look, or what they say about themselves, or that they smoke, or whatever. *What more?*

There is one class of women I've assiduously avoided, members of my tribe, namely Jewish women who, thanks to Match's religion-calibrated search function, I've excluded. I've given myself lots of reasons for this, including that I think that most Jewish women are overly demanding, hypercritical, judgmental, self-impressed, easily offended and ungrateful, and also unable to laugh at themselves, not to mention that they indulge Israel like parents laugh off the incorrigible acts of their children. But I'm open to the suggestion that Jewish women aren't all alike, that, in reality, I may be avoiding them for other less sustainable reasons, like that I'm the son of an awful one who married her age-reduced clone. Listening to myself, I do detect what may be a bit of deeply informed, narrowly drawn anti-Semitism.

Perhaps, I begin to think, I'm not properly weighing the adhesive value of shared culture? What about those shared nasal pathways that generate endorphin storms at the mere hint of a sourly pickled smell? And then there are those odd, 5,000-year-plus Jewish New Year holidays when we all swarm like it's Jewish census day. And don't we all mourn the disappearance of that Jewish cultural icon, the salty, somewhat chewy, definitely-not-sugary or raisin-imbued Jewish bagel, a holey bread that's both a major culinary achievement (setting the stage for important advances like whipped cream cheese and scallion-whitefish spread), and a shapely homage to that queen of Jewish-determining body parts, the vagina, the paramount Jewish edible.

So I lift my ban by adding "Jewish" to all the other religions of the world that I've already got checked in my Match search criteria, putting myself smack in the crosshairs of the lionesses of the Star of David pride.

She's already sitting at the table in Sushi Niji in affluent Alpine, New Jersey, where she's offered to meet. Her town, Whippany, is far away, so far that it's probably a good place for a truck stop on the Manhattan-Ohio route. Her head's slightly canted, cute and sly, going well with her long feline body that, thankfully, is quite similar to the one in the picture she posted on Match.

Far from saying that everyone thinks she's "perfect," or that she's been acclaimed the world's "greatest catch," her profile says that she's not that much of a Jew. She "observes the holidays," which, I'm hoping, is limited to the fake new year (Rosh Hashanah), begging to be left alive (Yom Kippur), and hurrah, no more pyramid-building, break out the funny-looking bread (Passover). She's "on a journey to places unknown," which I take to mean that, unlike her counterparts who say they most definitely know they're seeking men with pride, humility, genius, financial independence, courage, kindness, and the ability to keep the jokes coming, she doesn't know what she's looking for. That works because, frankly, I have no clue who I am or what I'm looking for.

"Any trouble finding the place?" she asks, extending a long-fingered, not excessively manicured hand that I shake. "Judy."

"Jed. That MapQuest is great," I say, looking around for something to look at, the menu, the Japanese waiters on the ready, anything to keep from staring at her.

"I know you haven't been divorced long," she says. "Are your kids handling it okay?"

The question surprises me, mainly because it's about me, about something that really is bothering me, something that, outside of AA, no one wants to listen to and, as a consequence, I've talked to almost no one about.

"They're in the middle. I'm probably prejudiced, but I think their mother is responsible for most of that, but I'm learning the limits of what I can do about it, and that's giving me a little more control over me making it worse. You?"

"I got bored. Fell out of love," she says, a bit embarrassed, very resigned, taking responsibility, no significant drama or effort to evade. She describes her ex as a "nice guy" whom she married when very young; their kids, though still in their teens, now, in her view, old enough to tolerate the fallout from her ending what had become, for her, quiet suffering, a charade.

The only thing that interrupts the flow of our disclosure is ordering, something I normally take as welcome relief from the tedium of asking questions I have no interest in knowing the answers to, and answering those I'm sorry have been asked. Now, though, I'm resenting this waiter who, though just doing his job, breaks our flow.

"À la carte sushi and sashimi?" I ask, tentatively, wondering if she'll share.

"Sure."

"You like *uni? Unagi?* Eel? Giant clam?"

"I like it all," she says, "except that fake crab shit. You order. Okay?"

The sushi and sashimi arrive, a giant platter, like a religious offering, a smorgasbord of Talmudic allergens weighing down the deck of a small, not-very-accurate but very clean model of a bamboo junk, piles of almost every non-kosher thing Jews have united in deriding since some ancient prophet killed the ghetto lobster business. She, my first Jewish date, dives in, even wrestling me for the last *uni*, delectable, orange, briny sea urchin sex organs, the best thing ever scraped from a verboten sea creature's shell, us agreeing to split it, splitting squishy delicate *uni* sushi though, unlike atoms, much like dating, very unscientific, but we try.

I'm not physically deconstructing her, which is good, and I'm getting lots of low-salt soy sauce in my lap because I'm nervous, a sign that I don't want to fuck this up, probably also good unless, of course, she doesn't like me the same way. I'm wondering, though, what exactly I like about her, a reasonable question that, strangely, I can't remember asking myself before, ever. Could this questioning be the effect of not drinking? Did alcohol and its socially lubricating effect shift me straight into sexual high gear, bypassing the lower speeds where, as I'm kind of awkwardly doing now, people assess the relationship's overall—sexual and otherwise—traction.

I like that she's sincere and cares about my answers, and that she speaks freely and honestly. But you can say that about anyone, and we all probably do at the beginning when people strike our fancy. They're all perfect—not boring, tedious, dissembling, two-faced, withholding, passive-aggressive, selfish, stuck-up, self-absorbed, thin-skinned, mean—until, of course, something goes wrong. But, alcohol or not, I've already got my head inside the undies clinging to those lean hips.

She likes ballet. Long and thin, she could pass for a former ballerina. And so we make a date to see Alvin Ailey, a dance company that, for the sake of my then-wife and a ballet-loving daughter, I've tried to like many times.

At a parking lot near City Center, she steps out of her car in an Italian knit dress showing enough long leg and highlighting enough chest to make me feel weak, like I'll never make it through the performance.

"Feeling okay?" she asks as we squeeze into our seats.

I appreciate how considerate she is and begin to explain my experience here last year, when my daughter didn't show. I sold her ticket at a steep discount to a daft old lady, not realizing that I'd just installed a lonely jabberwocky in a seat that would be adjoining mine for the entire performance, including three long intermissions.

"Yeah," I say, searching for something to follow with, something interesting, profound. Our shoulders rub, sort of on purpose.

"I like that," she whispers, smiling, I hope not noticing that I'm frozen, without an idea what to say.

"Feels good," she asks or states, I don't know which.

"I like you very much," I say, thinking I'm stammering and sounding very early pubescent.

"A little scary, right," she states or asks, the dimming lights saving me from figuring out an answer as she settles that beautiful, knit-ensconced ass into her seat, tapping my thigh, casting me a brief, mischievous look.

I do the long drive to Whippany and she answers the door at her ranch house, one that's empty of kids, the two of them with their father. Not wanting to leave my dog alone overnight, he's in tow, and I'm hoping he doesn't piss in her house. My arms are full of fresh basil and cherrystone clams and clam broth and pasta and heavy cream and Parmigiano-Reggiano, and all the other little ingredients of my clam sauce, which, I hope, does the aphrodisiacal trick.

"You bring everything. Nesting," she says coyly, a statement cum question, again I don't know which. "You're taking care of me. You should know I don't need it. But I like it."

I explore the kitchen, looking first for a pot to boil water in, something that doesn't look scavenged from a refugee camp, just, I think, a relatively flat bottom and only a few big dents. I find myself thinking that perhaps the lady doth protest too much about not needing help, at least insofar as kitchen utensils are concerned. Beyond a bit frustrating, it is, I think, cute, that everything in her kitchen either is chipped or doesn't work, the pasta strainer being thin, almost pancake-flat plastic, knives the likes of which I haven't seen since being in my now ex-mother-in-law's kitchen, where canned goods were arranged by decade, the knives, relics of gas station promotions, so dull none had an apparent cutting side.

We move in tandem down the hall towards the bedroom, neither hungry enough to want to eat first, me content letting broken utensils lie, my dog giving his wolfy bark, what he does when he sees people touching one another.

After, it having been wonderful, her being as beautiful as I had, by now, many times imagined, I couldn't help noticing that the bed we are lying on, essentially, is covered with a pile of old ragged linens. That is, there's no discernable top sheet, comforter, associated pillows. I wouldn't have given this much thought except for the fact that, when I reach behind my head to adjust my pillow, I find that my "pillow" is just a mound of crumpled sheets. Looking around, I see a creaky bedstand piled with old eyeglasses, and a dresser with two drawer faces falling off. And on my way to the bathroom, unable not to notice the wrinkled wall-to-wall carpeting that's lost its tuck, I'm told to use another bathroom because the bedroom one "isn't a good flush."

"You're thinking about making the clam sauce?" she whispers in my ear when I return.

Though I'm very hungry, the truth is that I'm actually thinking about what most interests me at this very moment, which is that there's cheap, broken stuff everywhere. There aren't any ceiling-high stacks of papers or magazines, so this isn't in the hoarding category. But she definitely has a problem passing the "25 Cents or Best Offer" tables at flea markets.

"Yeah," I say. "Hungry?"

"Go," she says. "You want to show me how good you are. Make this a home. You'll relax soon enough." She sends me off with an affectionate pat.

"Did you add this room?" I ask, us sitting in a cavernous family room disproportionately equal to the size of the remaining house, both of us slurping clam sauce, her with a properly formed soup spoon that I found after searching all the kitchen drawers. I'm doing my best with a twisted teaspoon with a loose enamel stem.

"We did. Yes. It's big. I know. You feel uncomfortable in here."

Again the questionable questions.

"It gives me space for my things," she continues. "I collect, you know."

"Collect?" I say, unable to suppress a small smile and chuckle.

"I know. I know. You like things in order. Open clean space. We're different. I'm not so concerned about losing things, everything being perfect."

I hear running water and, turning abruptly, I see my dog pissing on what looks like a leaning three-legged stool, probably once a full four-legged chair. I'm glad for the excuse to get up, which I do, gently but firmly disciplining him, cleaning the violated area, taking him out, walking the property, clearing my head. When I return, the dirty dishes are cleared and washed, clearing the path to another round of disheveled bed sex.

The "having of sex" with Judy, I realize in the weeks that follow, makes this weekend the inception point for mandatory nightly conversations confirming that we are now and continue to be an "us." Since long-distance calling now essentially is free, these conversations are omitted only at some risk. Today's "unlimited calling, texting, emailing," I realize, has had the unintended effect of making contact between insecure lovers mandatory every single fucking night.

We spend weekends alternating houses where we plan and execute "couples" activities, like lunch and dinner. She meets one of my children, the first to meet a girlfriend of mine, my daughter calling her "unconventionally pretty," the phrase making me proud to have an offspring who can turn one.

I definitely know I'm not "in love," but I am "in like," as in I mostly like spending time with Judy. She never stops explaining what I'm thinking and feeling, which makes me feel like I've got a TV shrink calling my psychological play-by-plays. This, in turn, makes me feel a bit muted, as in withholding thoughts so I don't get analyzed. Other than this, I am not too antsy. The sex still is regular and fun, and I've discovered the joys of a helpful little pill called Cialis that home delivers prescriptions that my brain writes but my body unreliably fills. I tell myself that this relationship is progress that I should hang on to.

And I'm content. Well, not exactly content. More like content, bored and restless, as in "Is this it?" This is my dominant thought, and it's only the early rounds. I don't remember feeling this way during the early years with my ex. Maybe back then we were stumbling along a different relational curve—distracted by developing professions, having babies, renovating apartments, picking schools, meeting everyone's expectations, assembling all the trappings of and doing all the things associated with young coupledom. Maybe back then all this now-completed marriagobilia monopolized the psychic stage, crowding out doubt, relegating ultimate questions to the rafters.

Now, though, whether this thing with Judy is *it* gnaws at me so much that I try on believing that it is, imagining her as my permanent relationship, my forever, taking on her voice, thoughts and obsession with cheap little broken things until one of us dies, the ecstatic end to online dating, the sex good all the time with this constant companion to whom I perpetually have to say "shhh" because she comments during movies. But this image produces what Judy would describe as feelings of fear and hopelessness, an analysis psychosomatically confirmed by heavy sweating.

I log on to Match, which, strangely, feels like taking a Xanax. Perusing feels even better, like a jailbreak. I click on an attractive dark siren, but she's a real estate broker, a profession whose members I can't stand listening to, on duty or off. Another cute one. No makeup. No strained poses. No admonitions about guys needing to "smell good" or make sure they're providing "recent photos" like hers. Hearing the rustle of bags and the chatter of teenagers, realizing that my three daughters have arrived for the week, I mark her as a Favorite to come back to and log off.

"Hey," Judy says to me on the phone around ten, the general nightly demark around which we jockey, waiting to see who calls first. Something about her "hey" sounds different. It isn't a happy "hey." But it isn't an angry "hey" either. It's more like a skeptical, kind of edgy "hey" that's missing the usual undertone of acceptance.

"Good timing," I say. "Just finished cleaning up from dinner. Kids are doing homework."

"Why are you on Match?" she asks, the generally benign façade I thought I was facing now a knife-studded board.

"Oh, um," I say, wanting a drink. "I, uh, went on just to tell a woman who I was emailing with before that I met someone. I'm involved with someone."

"We've been together for three months and you're 'Active Within 24 Hours,'" she says, referring to that thing on Match that tells you whether someone's "Active" or, instead, has taken a mental health break as indicated by not being online for "3 Days," or for a whole "Week" or, if really gonzo, "Not Since Al Gore Invented the Internet." But, I realize in a delayed flash of insight, she had to have been on Match to discover that I've been on Match, something I could've thrown back at her. In that case, I think, she'd probably say something like she missed me, wanted to see the old pictures, read the profile that drew her in, which, I realize, would have been a much better lie for me to have told, a very sensitive, relationship-affirming and flattering fib.

"Is that so?" she asks, her skeptical tone making me realize that I'm going to have to lay on a lot of lying drenched in insincere soul-searching to shore this one up. But why? We've never even discussed seeing other people much less agreed one way or the other. And why even discuss it, as it's only been three months? It's that thing, I guess. The sex thing. That thing that changes everything, like you've both just won Olympic gold medals for pairs skating or shared a Nobel for psychodynamics when, in fact, you've barely tried on the skates or cracked the psych book. Isn't sex just a step, an aspect, an experience, one of the underpinnings on which love can develop, or not?

"What are you really asking?" I ask.

"Well, we haven't discussed much of this."

"*This* being?"

She doesn't answer, not right away, not apparently intending to at all. Long silences, I notice, are more bearable on the phone than in person.

"If you want to know if I'm still looking around, just ask me," I say, wondering why on earth I'm pressing her to ask me a question I don't want to answer, knowing that this line of questioning only leads someplace where I won't need Cialis.

"We can just be friends, then," she says.

"Friends?"

"Get together," she says. "Have dinner."

"Judy. You live two hours away," I say, trying to stop myself, which I can't. "You know what asking me to make a four-hour round-trip for dinner means?"

As I'm saying this I'm asking myself, *Why am I doing this?* I had a perfectly good lie going, one I could have improved. And if lying made me too uncomfortable, since I hadn't yet committed any kind of overt act—like contacting someone—I always could have owned up to what's sort of the truth, that the closeness was making me nervous, what with my last mistake costing me twenty-three years. Judy surely is the kind of person who'd analyze the entire course of conduct, revel in my honest disclosure and growing self-awareness, concluding that, if anything, I'm taking our relationship seriously, the historical evidence being that I'm not a commitment-phobe.

"I know," she says. "But I'm not sleeping with someone who's looking around."

Fair enough, I think, because I don't think I'd want to be on the other end of that. But I just can't bring myself to say it, to accept what appears to be an offer to put the wheels back on the relationship, set things sort of straight.

"We're just getting to know each other," I say, again pushing towards the loneliness end zone.

"And that can continue," she says, "but as friends."

This, I know, is the ultimatum, one I have to accept willingly, meaning quickly, or it's going to be withdrawn on the ground that the passage of time means I'm too equivocal, fickle, flaky, possibly responding favorably only because my arm's being twisted and, thus, evidently insincere. *Say the words,* I think. *Say them now. Admit mistake. Plead for understanding. Beg for help.* But nothing comes out.

So I'm left holding the phone, which feels like holding the bag. After overplaying to get women, I underplay to keep them, but why? Am I too critical? Not picky enough? Too easily bored? Absorbed in my own world? Wanting a lot? Not needy enough? Afraid of something? Or is all this just a bunch of bobbing and weaving to avoid facing something deeper, more complex, perhaps irresolvable?

STUCK IN THE PASSING LANE

I'm boiling in my own oils in the hot tub behind the tract house I just hastily purchased. Afraid that my daughters might stop visiting the farmhouse, I rammed this purchase through, thirty days from seeing to closing. Though the kids initially overlooked the isolated mouse or spider in the farmhouse, the regular appearances of these pests during the past six months made infestation undeniable. But I'm not sure buying this house was the greatest idea because, with the twins leaving for college shortly, and the youngest opting to stay mainly at her mother's, soon I'll be plodding down this split-level's low-ceiling, resoundingly empty hallways alone, like Jack Nicholson in *The Shining*.

I'm turning up the jets, wondering about all these failed attempts at coupling. Actually, I'm blaming myself for barreling through relationships, punting or becoming disenchanted at the slightest sign of being pestered. This must be sobriety. Taking responsibility.

Looking beyond the surface. The route to becoming relationship-capable.

Being alone seems so much easier. I recently read that the monogamous relationship may have been designed to last only for the duration of the once drastically shorter human lifespan. Maybe we simply age-out of relationships now that we live so long. If so, when that period ends, with novelty receding and pesky routine setting in, do the more mature among us just double down with the devil we know, perhaps the only person in the world who one day may be willing to push our wheelchair and change our diapers?

I know this just can't be what it all means. Am I wanting too much? Clinging to a childish fantasy? The male version of those Match women who warn that you'd better be terrific because they *won't settle*? Am I in that subset of humanity that would rather wake up to emailed *billet-doux* representing endless possibilities than roll over against the same muss-haired, croaky-voiced adjoining body?

Perhaps, though, the problem is me in a different sense: that I'm just picking the wrong women. I decide to talk this over with Steven, a long-divorced guy I recently met while walking Kobi. Steven's *experienced*; he's practically a founding member of Match. I dial him from the hot tub on my cell phone.

"Steven?"

"You just caught me. I'm heading for San Francisco," Steven answers.

"Why San Francisco?" I ask. His trip seems a little late, what with Jerry Garcia dead, Haight-Ashbury gentrified, Mama Cass having succumbed to the ultimate weight-loss plan.

"I found her."

"In San Francisco?"

"Yeah. We're inseparable. I'm going out to meet her."

"How can you be inseparable when you've never met?"

Steven doesn't answer. I assume that's because he doesn't want to consider whether, as with most Match dates, his ballooning infatuation is about to meet reality's cold, cruel pinprick.

"Who is she?"

"She's thirty-nine. A psychologist with her own small practice. No kids. Never married but some long relationships."

"How did you find her?"

"I did a nationwide Match search, and there she was."

"A nationwide search for what?"

"I just put it all out there. Everything I want: Jewish. Graduate degree. Under forty. Doesn't want kids."

"That's it?" I ask, thinking how many great women aren't Jewish or are but lack graduate degrees. And what of all of the U.S.'s single Jewish women with graduate degrees—a number I'd guess is in the hundreds of thousands? How did Steven use Match's search capability to exclude those who listen to Suze Orman? Who read Eckhart Tolle? Who have spiritual lives that are *active,* like yeast?

"There she was. Jumped right up."

"Well, good luck," I say.

Not yet willing to throw in the towel, I head for my computer. I switch on Match and begin culling women by age, height and body type, then selecting divorced nonsmokers not wanting kids, looking through the photos that even slightly appeal to me. I chastise myself for being as careless and non-deliberative in picking women as I've recently been in selecting houses, though the latter at least is somewhat justified by a dearth of choices. But then I remember the sculptor Henry Moore saying something about his art involving "chipping away at what isn't." That's my method too, I think, as I hone in on an attractive woman who doesn't live far, the residue of the process of elimination wielded by a guy exhausted from moving.

I'm feeling it with Sharon, forty-nine, older than I'm used to but, in the light emitted by the candles I've lit in my den, waifishly sexy with long, straight black hair falling over her shoulders and down her back. It's feeling intimate already, like it's the third date, the important decision imminent, her moving next to me, touching my forearms and shoulders, giving affectionate "get out of here" soft palm pushes to my chest, a sign it's a go.

Having waived the requisite inquisition about past relationships, what passed for conversation during our earlier dinner mainly was moaning about the taste of one another's food that we shared with communal forks, feet and knees brushing, flirting eyes meeting, her air so permissive that I made a purely second date move, sliding my hand under hers.

"Do you want me to go home after?" she asks amidst short, sweet lip-brushing kisses.

"No," I say, my thinking compromised by the pleasure of pulling her sweater over her head, untangling her hair and earrings, freeing small, soft breasts that the shadows cast in a larger light.

We continue the evening's conversational track, moaning and dispensing with questions, including about condoms and STDs, me assuming her recently concluded, long marriage mitigates my risk. I fuck her on the brown Bob's Discount Furniture sectional, christening it, learning the hard way that a sectional is made of, well, *sections* that, under pressure, slide apart, wondering if her being so wet will stain the corduroy, kicking myself for not getting the thing Scotchgarded.

Cold creeps up on us. I consider bringing down the comforter from the bedroom but, wanting to seem a gentleman, instead invite her up. I bring our clothes, hoping she'll soon be wearing hers out.

She snuggles into the traditional post-intercourse position, the one in which the woman tries to extend the previous intimacy, me on my back, her head and arms cuddling hard into my chest, my arm, intimidated, enwrapping her.

"Do you jerk off much?" she asks.

"What?"

"You know," she says.

"Do you?" I ask.

"Of course, and with toys. Do you watch porn?"

"I have a few," I say, *no* being too obvious a lie. If she asks me to put one on I plan to say that I'm not sure which box they're in; no encore for me.

"You ate me really nice. I came when you were doing that, you know?"

Why do I feel like I'm being interviewed for a job I already have? Or is this macho sex talk her way of trying to switch attention from our signs of age, now showing in the post-sex glare, to how experienced she is. I go through my equivalent, overly complimenting the great sex to cover up that I ain't getting it up again anytime soon.

"What's your fantasy?" she asks, pushing intimacy that's pushing me away.

"I don't know."

"You must have one," she insists and, to move on, I make one up.

"Oh, I think it would be very sexy to have someone surprise me at the front door in a fur coat and, underneath, they're naked."

"I could do that," she says, nestling in.

"It's winter, honey. Too cold," I say, getting up, saying I've got to walk my dog, dressing and, in the guise of being neat, arranging her clothes on the bed, not in a heap, but in the order someone would put them on.

"Don't you have dog?" I ask. "It's been like six hours. Doesn't your dog—"

"He's in the basement," she says. "He'll—"

"Shit there?"

"Yeah," she says, dressing, refusing my bedroom-departing hug, but accepting Kobi and me accompanying her to the driveway.

In the morning I get an email from Sharon apologizing for being so unfriendly, saying she had a nice evening, likes me and hopes we give things a chance.

The boyfriend reshaping part of me keeps me from doing what I want, which is forgetting about Sharon, absconding. It's forcing me instead to make an effort to understand her, translating her email. Not immediately giving up is, I find, a bit easier for a strange reason—that she apologized. The apology astonishes me until I realize that I can't remember my ex ever apologizing for anything, not even in that gratuitous, unmeant way we all do to signal concern, or at least brinksmanship.

The translation, though, is unnerving. It means she likes me far more than I know I'll ever like her. If I were the stud I aspire to be, which experience is telling me I'm not, that would be cool; I'd add Sharon to the others whose affections I'd manipulate and relationships I'd juggle—Cara the Puerto Rican, Judy the unconventionally pretty woman. But the software in my stud module apparently is blown.

"Why don't you do Russian babes?" asks Jeffrey, one of our trio of Madison Square Garden Knicks game *floppers,* the other being Larry. I've been friends with Larry for a little over two months. About a month before leaving the farmhouse, I swore I'd befriend whomever came through the door next, an anti-loneliness vow of sorts. Larry, an accepting, older, seemingly successfully remarried guy arrived to fix the burglar alarm and, so, he became new friend number one.

"He's not going to do *that,*" says Larry, giving the long-term married guy's answer to the committed bachelor Jeffrey's very interesting suggestion. The two men, so different in many respects, share the thrill of "flopping," which, generally, is stealing expensive seats at Knicks games, a feat accomplished by getting ushers comfortable enough with you to accept your twenty-dollar bribe to sit in a vacant three-hundred-dollar-seat with your twenty-five-dollar ticket.

"Who's paying Wally?" Jeffrey asks, referring to the obligatory mid-fourth period trek up the stadium steps to discreetly palm three twenties into the usher-of-the-day's downturned hand.

"You mean Charlie," Larry says.

"No, it's Wally," Jeffrey insists. This is not an empty tiff. They usually bicker over the usher's name because knowing the name proves who *owns* the usher. Owning bribe-accepting ushers, like politicians, indicates rising status in the seat-stealing mafia (the usher's name, by the way, is Willie, and he's mine).

With Jeffrey heading up to give Willie his cash, I make small talk with the woman seated next to him. She's beautiful, olive-skinned, black perm-haired and thirtyish, sitting alone, paying no attention to the game, texting. Sporting events are a relatively new pick-up venue for me. It started with the U.S. Open tennis tournament last summer where I dreamt up buying adjoining seats and giving one to the cutest girl alone in the ticket buyers' line. The recipient, a Hungarian dermatologist, unfortunately, was departing that evening, or so she said after Federer won in straight sets.

"Knicks suck, right?" I say, come-on lines in Madison Square Garden being easy to come by. The din, the makeup of the crowd and, of course, the consensus about this incredibly overpriced, incredibly fucked-up basketball team, dictating the subject.

"They're okay," she says. "They need some time."

"Here alone?" I ask, emboldened by her slightly more than just perfunctory response.

"That's my boyfriend," she says, pointing to a six-ten power forward just then pounding up the court like a *Jurassic Park* T-Rex.

Home, I'm checking out Jeffrey's idea, exploring websites with lots of exquisite Russian women photographed on the sexually charged edge of feigned modesty. About 80 percent of these women conveniently bear one of six names (Tatiana, Svetlana, Anastasia, Olga, Natalya, Galina), the standardizing of the names of women now in their thirties, I'm guessing, reflecting now-disfavored Soviet central planning. Then I see an advertisement for a book called *How to Get a Girl Like Me for Your Wife* by Ms. Danika Annikova. "Search for Russian wife is science! Find out how! Don't waste time and money!" Ms. Danika, mistress of exclamation marks, exclaims:

> *Leave your competition behind you. Attract Russian woman like fly to honey. Understand their minds. What they want and how to give it to them so they believe you.*
>
> *Look at my picture. For almost nothing, you can find out how to marry girl just like this!*

The referenced picture is of a woman with a body that looks as awesome as the young Jane Fonda did in *Barbarella*, plus long, wavy chestnut hair, legs that could enwrap beer barrels and an enticing look I've seen only one other place on earth: the Red Light District in

Amsterdam. I pay the $29.99 for the how-to book fast, like it's a bridge toll.

Ms. Danika's also into repetition. These women, Ms. Danika repeats more ways than a thousand-dollar-a-night hooker can get you off, are not economic refugees. They're not materialistic. They're imbued with soul, proud, highly educated and very cultured. Sincere, cordial, understanding and unselfish, they'd all much rather stay in that godforsaken, economically desperate, mafia-run, skinhead-ridden, loose-nuke-containing corrupt police state called Russia. The only little problem, Ms. Danika says, is that Russian shelves are groaning under the weight of a surfeit of marriage-age women, and Russian men mainly are cheating, abusive, drunken fools no self-respecting woman with half a brain would ever marry.

Buried in *How to Get a Girl Like Me for Your Wife* I find two more facts that set off Boston Pops Fourth of July Sousa marches in my head, driving me towards these Tatianas like a heat-seeking ABM. Middle-aged U.S. men like me, Ms. Danika correctly assesses, want women in their thirties, a problem because, in the U.S., women in their thirties want kids (which I can't give), and don't want older guys (which I am). Russian women, Ms. Danika says, don't mind older guys. Better, they're not looking to get their eggs fertilized because, generally, by their early twenties, husband or not, they've already arranged that, each having at least one neat little kid.

I call Ms. Danika's www.danikasrussianbeauties.com 800 number, wanting to learn how to do this fast and get way out in front on the Anastasia-hunting curve. A woman named Anna answers. We establish good rapport immediately, owing to both of us fending off our dogs, mine begging for breakfast, hers, eight hours ahead in Moscow, awaiting dinner.

Anna has what I'd loosely call an "I'll suck your dick off your balls" Russian accent. My hopes now controlling my reactions, I find this accent sexy rather than suspicious. Anna recommends paying a thousand dollars to expedite these transactions, for which I get unlimited back-and-forth email translations, access to her *private stock* of women too good for the website, her excellent advice and some other "wait, wait . . . that's not all" stuff. Though the whole thing sounds like a late-night TV hoax, with my dick now suspending my brain's reasonable disbelief, I immediately accept, wiring the grand. My increasingly active dream life tonight generates one of me frantically selling all my stocks and bonds, converting everything into cash, then rubles.

I'm working back and forth with Anna, me creating, her editing and translating what Mel Brooks would call *History of Jed, Part I*, an enticement written according to Ms. Danika's often-contradictory rules for finding a girl like her. Don't appear too materialistic or try to impress her with your wealth, but "if you own a house, tell about it" but be cool:

> *"I own a huge house" will sound better if you say, "My house is nice with much space for visitors, such as if anybody of your family comes to stay."*

Don't promote yourself too openly, remembering, though, that Russian women "in general don't like men who nobody want" which, translated, means make them think you're the greatest thing since smelly little fish eggs got rebranded as caviar. Make sure what you say about them shows that you "appreciate their nature and character," and never say they're "gorgeous" because that would suggest that "you just like their physical," in other words, the truth. "Be yourself," says Ms. Danika, and express your personality, because "a girl sees lying." But don't write about anything that matters, no problems, and especially not your divorce:

> ***What never to write about****: your ex-wife and any bad natures of her or how she is crazy or hurts you or your kids, your problems with love, women or life in general, anything sexual, losing your hair, health problems (except say if you are in a wheelchair, are paralyzed in any way, have artificial limbs, or lack any important capacities due to an accident or sickness; otherwise she will feel cheated).*

Wait to tell her these things after she knows you enough to trust you a little, and tell them to her face so you can see what her feeling.

Lastly, and what a little voice tells me isn't the least, you must "express your heart and soul rather than be correct," which, with my new Russian profile height of five-eight now more accurately reflecting my innate stature than my nominal five-six in shoes, I totally get.

While constructing my story, I'm also working the Danika's Russian Beauties website, a vast quarry of Anastasias and Natalyas, no stone in which I want to leave unturned. Suddenly, I realize this website's extra special advantage: it's a refuge from American women you're dating, none of whom would ever think to look for you looking here.

The doorbell in the split-level rings. This is only the second time I've heard it, the first being Jehovah's Witnesses, the only unsolicited visitors motivated enough to make their way down my long driveway.

"Hi," Sharon says. Something about her chipper smile and how she's wrapping her arms around herself to keep her fur coat closed makes me uncomfortable.

"Did you say you were coming over?" I ask, thinking this is a date I've forgotten.

"No," she says, stepping past me into the foyer, exclaiming "surprise" from behind.

I know I have to turn around and face her, but I don't want to. Really badly I don't want to. It's like I just accidentally sliced deeply into my finger and this is that fretful, painless second before the blood flows and the agony hits.

"Oh," I manage to say, though I know I have to add more. "More" is difficult to come by though, but I try, my technique being to imagine what I look like naked, my unsucked-in potbelly, the oily glint off the substantial scalp area normally covered by my toupee, the eye bags no longer allayed by rest, hair growing up my neck. But the sight of her in her birthday suit in daylight, saggy flesh, splotchy skin, coat at her feet, paralyzes me.

I force a smile as she waits, expecting, I think, a huge *thank you* for delivering my supposed fantasy, the one I made up to get her off my back.

"Aren't you cold?" I ask, rewrapping and ushering her upstairs, where I re-unwrap and quickly place her under the comforter.

"Just give me a minute," I say, excusing myself for the bathroom where I frantically search for the fast-acting Viagra pill someone once gave me. Her expecting me to be as hard as a suicide bomber receiving his seventy virgins just doesn't leave enough time for slower-acting Cialis.

I slide in next to her, limp as a room-temperature raw sausage, her ice-cold skin not helping the process. I'm trying to stay behind her, spooning, rubbing up against her, creating some warmth against which I can grow, but she turns over, making eye contact, what women think makes sex more than, well, sex. Now, despite window treatments supposedly blocking out 80 percent of the light, I can clearly see features that I was able to overlook, or looked better in candlelight. *What do my acne scars look like up close in this light? Do these shades really block 80 percent? Was the window shade sales guy bullshitting me?*

It's coming on twenty minutes, and I'm still limp. She throws off the blanket and gets up. The gulf between how hot she thinks she's being and my complete lack of erogenous response is fast becoming a statement to her about us. Though I beg her to wait, to help, I can't stop her from putting on her coat and storming out. *Shit*, I think. *Why don't male genitals have their own version of the vagina's "poker face"?*

BEHIND THE IRON CURTAIN'S GREEN DOOR

I'M FOCUSING IN ON Larisa, one of Anna's special crew. She's thirty-nine with an eight-year-old child. She's beautiful, with flowing red hair and striking blue eyes, but a bit stiff looking, the latter probably reflecting her discomfort posing in these self-marketing photos. Fluent in English and holding doctorates in both political science and economics, she works for a Russian think tank that, if I'm reading the English version of its website correctly, is kind of a cross between the left-leaning Brookings Institution and the right-wing Heritage Foundation. She seems perfect for me: she's attractive and we have common interests, like English.

With the help of a cheap phone card, we're talking every day, my mornings to her evenings as she's eight hours ahead. She's so interested in perfecting her English, which is almost always correct but a bit rigid, that she's constantly asking me to explain English idioms and slang I don't even realize I'm using. And so, when I gently slide a conversation about verb conjugation into wordplay about physical activity that also falls within the meaning of that verb, she gets it. Giggling, pausing, shyly she tells me that someday she'll make me "eat those words."

Though we quickly finish the basics—prior relationships, childrearing, family—we don't run out of things to talk about. I'm now reading everything I can find about Russia, from Hedrick Smith's *The Russians* to David Remnick's *Lenin's Tomb*, learning about what's happened through Glasnost and Perestroika, the huge suffering and dislocation, the starvation in major cities like Moscow. Like a good political scientist, she easily moves from discussing these big political and economic events to personal stories about how they affected her and her family. We trade more photos, her sending me profiles in quarter-inch turns, while I send comic poses: at Columbus Circle making it seem I'm holding aloft the steel globe outside the Trump Hotel; in a children's playground atop a hippopotamus; on a bronze bench chatting with cast bronze elderly people. She shares upcoming subjects she'll be researching: Russia's inexcusably inhumane orphanage system, the risks associated with having an oil-sector-dominated economy, interviews with entrepreneurs about Russian red tape. After two months of this intense communication, sensing us drawing close enough to consider scheduling a visit, I enroll in basic Russian at NYU.

One November night, she tells me that she and her daughter Marta are taking the overnight train to St. Petersburg that Friday to visit some relatives, returning late Sunday evening. Saturday, I call my Russian matchmaker, Anna, to find out when the late train from St. Petersburg arrives in Moscow Sunday night, and to find out about the weather, Moscow and St. Petersburg being about the same latitude as Oslo and Stockholm, places where winter is rough. Allowing an hour for the subway ride from the train station, and another hour for the long walk home from the subway, I calculate they should be getting to their front door just after midnight her time, which is when I call.

"Larisa?"

"Jed?"

"Are you and Marta okay?"

"We are walking in the cold and the snow," she says, illustrating a propensity of hers that I've noticed for elevating suffering and threats to conversational first place, as in "We are poor" when describing why they don't have some common household item, or "Bread is enough" when lamenting the effort required to go food shopping, or calling the vegetable and fruit sellers in the nearby market "thieves." I don't know if this is a Larisa or a Russian thing. Their decades of deprivation make me think it's the latter. Perhaps due to their ubiquity, their discomforts can monopolize conversations, much like medical conditions seem to be all that older Floridians talk about.

"How long until you get home?"

"I don't know. Marta wants me to carry her. But I have our bags."

"Why don't you take a taxi?"

"No taxis."

"Call me on my phone card when you get home?"

"Yes."

"Okay, well . . ."

"Jed, you call us. You watch over us. So I know you care for us."

Here's a woman who makes a living and supports a child in a country that oligarchs run like a piggy bank, where the government and the authorities are mafia-like criminal enterprises, and where the social safety net is a breadline if you can find one and a relative who'll let you and your kid crash on the sofa. This strong-willed woman hardened by a life spent defending her and her child with nothing but intelligence, street smarts, hard work and common sense, remains soft enough to appreciate a privileged-ass American like me taking a minute to check up on her from five thousand miles away?

That's different. I'm hooked.

I'm in Bloomingdale's, supplementing my current wardrobe, which consists of a T-shirt for every occasion, with clothing suggested on Ms. Danika's laundry list of what the appropriately costumed American needs to wear to shanghai a Russian woman: a stylish winter coat, two sport jackets, snazzy slacks, fashionable shirts and pullovers, sweaters, new ties and boots for the Russian winter. For all this, I'm being Armani'd, Polo'd, Boss'd, Lacoste'd and UGG'd by *Fräulein* Gabriele, my German saleswoman who patiently matches clothes, deciding what I need to avoid being seen in the same thing two days in a row. She arranges tailoring and delivery, sending me to her counterparts on other floors for Tumi luggage, and the cologne that Ms. Danika says is a *sine qua non* of male eligibility to Russian women. On the business card she hands me she writes her cell number and a note wishing me *many happy returns.* I don't know if she means with Larisa or more buying trips to the store.

Departing in forty-eight hours, my emotions, previously anesthetized by the pressure of completing all these preparations, awaken. As they do, I wonder why the fuck I'm going all the way to Russia to test a relationship with someone from a completely different culture that I'll have ten days to gauge. Why, with all of the single available women right here, am I gambling all this time, money and emotion on someone whose immigration issues alone make Hannibal's problems getting his army across the Alps look like a domestic ski vacation? Does it make any sense to test a relationship with someone who I can only get to know by making a premature commitment, like bringing her here where she'll know no one and won't be able to work in her profession, and where she'll be entirely dependent on the world's most supportive, human interaction guru—yours truly?

This isn't rational. It's an entirely unnecessary, desperate act justifiable only if I accept the absurd proposition that, ultimately, every U.S. woman will disappoint me, and that Russia's borders contain hordes of women offering a more enduring and acceptable form of love than I can find here.

I'm struggling to feel positive, to reduce all these anticipated headwinds to mere puffs of nervous anticipation. I feed myself a myth about how far I've already come Larisa-acquainting and Russian dating-wise. It makes it easier for me to fool myself into ignoring how wacked out this is.

Now I'm imagining how bad it will be if, as is entirely possible, Larisa and I don't get along. That will make my ten days in Moscow feel like the Siberian winter Omar Sharif went through chasing the young Julie Christie in *Dr. Zhivago*, without Julie Christie. Though it's probably bad luck to think things won't work out, I decide to do some damage control, find a backup.

I must do this deftly, I think, meaning so that matchmaker Anna doesn't learn about it. I know that a Russian woman who's been individually romanced, as I have Larisa, will take Stalin-size offense at being treated like inventory. Anna will tell Larisa, the two circling their smoke-chugging Volgas, leaving me out in the Moscow cold. So I settle on Galina, a woman I meet through another Russian dating website where I won't be tracked by Larisa or Anna unless, of course, they're ex-KGB.

Galina, a translator for McDonald's Russian corporate headquarters, has long dark hair and a bacchanalian propensity, her theme song, I'm guessing, is "Girls Just Want to Have Fun." Galina's *fun,* according to her mono-topic emails, is partying every fucking minute she can pawn her kid off on her mother. Galina and I agree to have dinner the first night I arrive, which is in just two days. I arrange to meet Larisa for the first time the morning after I see Galina when, I claim, I won't be so jetlagged. Packing the condoms beside the cologne, then moving them for fear the cologne, though double-bagged, might leak, I think *Galina, she'll protect me from becoming the Guinness World Record holder for biggest effort ever expended not getting laid.*

Heading for the airport, I make a last call to matchmaker Anna, saying goodbye, getting her good luck wishes, asking her to let Larisa know that I'm really only four feet tall, a joke her audible gasp says she doesn't realize is a joke, her reaction, she explains, being because "now is when all the lies come out."

I'm in a window seat on the flight from JFK to Moscow's Sheremetyevo International Airport, spinning the barrel with Aeroflot, Russia's unstable national airline that offers cheap business-class seats, the aeronautical version of the Russian roulette I'm playing on the ground. I'm wondering why they don't call Sheremetyevo something easier on the international traveler's tongue and ear, a Russian version of Reagan or Kennedy or Dulles or O'Hare, not Dostoyevsky, not Gorbachev nor Yeltsin, maybe Tolstoy or Chekhov or, yes, Uncle Vanya International.

Looking around the cabin, trying to pick out the Russian women, I'm wondering why I'm heading for the insobriety capital of the universe during Christmas and New Year's, high season for drunks. Celebrating my one year of sobriety in a city synonymous with the opposite is kind of like starting Weight Watchers at a sumo wrestler fattening camp. I'm hoping that what I've been told—that there are English-speaking AA meetings in almost every major city—applies to Moscow despite its recent meteoric tumble down the list of the world's great metropolises.

Nickolai, unshaven, is my matchmaking service-supplied escort, ferrying me from Sheremetyevo to my hotel, the Metropol Moscow, from whose balcony, the tour book says, Lenin rallied the proletariat. On the drive in, I decline Nickolai's offer to be my private chauffeur for the trip. Nickolai goes silent, speaking again only when we pass a steel marker very close to town that, he says, marks where the Russians stopped the Nazi blitzkrieg on Moscow.

STUCK IN THE PASSING LANE

"One thing," Nickolai says, navigating the guards and concrete barriers blocking the way into the parking area. "Here man decides and tells woman what to do." I ponder this somewhat revisionist approach to male-female relations as Nickolai removes my bags, closes the trunk and lights a cigarette. "But then she decides," he adds, this being the somewhat cryptic conclusion to his highly distilled summary of Cyrillic homelife.

Valets in wrinkled, uncoordinated uniforms are lounging in front of the massive white-brick hotel. One grabs my Tumi luggage. Not entirely trusting him, I follow my bags and their carrier into the Metropol. It's the Russian version of New York's Grand Central Station, what I'd call the "Vast Siberian Steppes" style. The lobby, an empty football stadium, my room, a practically unfurnished apartment awaiting a new tenant.

I'm not feeling openness and, in fact, I feel like I've been dropped into a Lucite box filled with seawater. Maybe fear's taking hold. More likely, I think, it's the hardened looks of the desk clerks, cleaners, valets, concierges, looks that may just be the normal Russian "hard smile" that I read about in a magazine, smiles that restaurateurs here have to teach their employees to soften.

I feel like I'm facing a battery of "I hate you" smiles whose forced, barely upturned corners say that this hate isn't superficial, that it runs deep and is expanding exponentially, reproducing like an infection under ideal conditions. I sense huge inferiority complexes, deep resentments about unappreciated scientific and cultural achievements, festering shame over their country's fall to failed-African-state status, smoldering anger at living where only corrupt officials and mafioso can afford decent lifestyles, and massive offense at having to smile at the embodiment of all they hate—a rich American—to get their nonliving wage and, if they're lucky, a tip.

I need air, and there is still a bit of daylight. The Kremlin, per the map, is nearby. I decide to take a walk, crossing the walled-in parking lot, passing bulky chauffeurs smoking, leaning against black Mercedes. It's unclear where the sidewalk is because not much attention has been paid to clearing snow and ice. I feel much colder than I'd expect on a calm day with the temperature around freezing. Maybe it's the pervasive moisture. The cold dampness is penetrating deeply, like wet blankets wrapped around naked people left in cold cellars, a thought that I'm sure occurred to Dick Cheney as he added this torture technique to the list of what he thinks *doesn't* violate the Geneva Accords.

I'm the only pedestrian until a guy I didn't even hear coming speeds by, sound probably muffled by the snow. As he passes, a roll of dollars bound with a rubber band falls out of his pocket into the snow. I grab the wad and run after him, tapping him on the shoulder, offering the bills. Fast as a guillotine, a hand belonging to a guy in a brown uniform grabs my hand holding the bills. The guy in the uniform is wearing a furry hat with four flaps tied up, with a big red star pinned to the one facing me.

"Passport," says this Russian policeman, his clipped tone suggesting he isn't on tourist-helping duty today.

The guy who lost the money is looking at the cop and doesn't look at me. The cop is waiting and, I think, isn't going to wait much longer. The whole thing—the money dropping next to me, the cop appearing out of nowhere, the guy to whom I'm being a good Samaritan not saying so—all seems kind of fishy but, then, this is Russia, where, I've heard, official fishiness is *de rigueur*. My heart pounds while my brain runs through the possibilities: give him my passport and get it back and be let go; give him my passport and not get it back; offer him twenty and either get the passport back or be taken in for bribery. Oh, and on the possibility that he isn't a cop, maybe make a run for it, which, if he really is a cop, will turn the hopefully modest Russian offense of giving someone back the money they dropped into a Chernobylesque street crime.

When the cop glances over at the other guy, I give him a two-handed shove, creating enough space for me to start running towards the hotel. I'm running, but not too fast because I'm on ice and snow, not looking back, expecting momentarily to be tackled. Passing through the hotel's concrete block perimeter, I keep going until, glancing back, I see that no one's chasing me. Resting in the lobby on a plump, garish red loveseat at the base of an equally garish globed two-story brass lamp, I discover that something wonderful has happened: in this once-suffocating space, I am, albeit rapidly and shallowly, breathing.

During a well-deserved shower, I decide that I'm too obviously a tourist, owing to coming out of the Metropol, and probably dressing in a way that flashes "I'm a foreigner, rip me off." Tomorrow, I'll buy one of those furry four-flapped hats, maybe with a red star. I'll wear it the way I've seen the Russians do, way down on the eyebrows, low-riding, like the hat's cruising in an old Camaro.

It's 8 p.m. and I'm in the lobby dressed in my new Armani tweed jacket, my new Ralph Lauren Polo blue knit shirt, my new Hugo Boss brown slacks and some old brown shoes, all for Galina, my backup date to Larisa, who thinks I'm too tired to see her for the first time until tomorrow. I feel like Dustin Hoffman, toothbrush in breast pocket, waiting for Anne Bancroft in *The Graduate*. However, Galina's arrival, announced by a commotion at the door, is far less discreet than Mrs. Robinson's.

I wait while the doormen and security guards struggle, all trying to force my date towards the manager's desk. I gather from the desk clerk that, according to everyone, including the desk clerk, who doesn't know she's with me, she's a whore. The giveaway, I'm guessing, assuming Russian hoteliers don't assume that all single women are prostitutes, is that she's wearing what they think is the Russian whore uniform: head-to-toe fur, including a white silver fox sailor boy hat with silver foxtail tassels, a silver fox boa, a white silky dress with silver fox cuffs and hem, a silver fox-lined plummeting neckline, and tall stiletto pumps accented with, yes, foxy pieces.

"She's with me," I tell the manager. Galina and I appraise one another. The circumstances, despite being somewhat similar to those already reprised in *Pretty Woman*, are uncomfortable.

"She must leave her passport to go up to the rooms," the manager says. The way he uses the plural "rooms" starts to really piss me off. Based on my now extensive experience with the Russian people, this recurrent *passport* thing, I'm thinking, is really just a euphemism for bribery, these efforts being to ensure that the underpaid staff get their fair share of Galina's anticipated gains.

"She is my guest," I say adamantly. "We're having dinner here."

"Yes. But she still must leave her passport."

"You'll return it when she leaves, no trouble?"

"Trouble? No trouble," he says, sarcastically pausing on each word, his tone so reeking of disingenuousness that it would belie any claim that I believed what he just said. As Galina relinquishes her passport, I'm wondering whether he'll be here when we return, and what if it's tomorrow morning.

I'm pretty good with small talk, but it just isn't that easy conjuring up an opening line with someone you're meeting for the first time when it's just been broadcast that she's a prostitute, nothing about her indicating otherwise. I quickly reject old stalwarts: "Did you get here okay?" "Lovely hotel, isn't it?" "Your people are so friendly." And, of course, "Nice weather. Is it typical?"

"Sorry about that," I say, which I believe is kind of how the very suave Richard Gere smoothed things over with the as-kinky-as-wholesome-allows Julia Roberts in *Pretty Woman*.

"Are you hungry?"

"Yes," she says, giving me the first smile I've seen since the Aeroflot staff said goodbye on the plane. With that, I escort her towards the back of the lobby, where I hope there's a restaurant.

Galina's ordering almost everything on the menu, not all that much since it's a very short list, from tortured-looking little pickled river fish, to sour-creamy mystery-meat gruel, tiny servings on huge plates, the culinary display reinforcing my evolving sense of Russia where value, warmth and friendliness are spread thinly, like caviar.

"So tonight, yes, a *dacha*, no?" Galina says, caressing with her finger a small beauty mark on her milky white breast.

"A *dacha*?"

"Yes. A house in the, you know, trees," she says.

I tilt my head a bit and raise my eyebrows, what I hope is the international look for not understanding,

"The *koontree*. Party. Cool people," she says.

"Oh, yes. A country house. Is it far?" I ask, adding quickly, so as not to seem unenthusiastic, "I mean, how do we get there?"

"My friends, they drive," she says. "Lots of vodka. The holidays, yes? In the U.S. too?"

I have this picture in my head of me in a tumbledown house in the middle of nowhere. Though reminiscent of my hippie-commune days, this one doesn't contain tripping flower children bent on making love not war. It's filled with big, hairy biker wannabes and gene-pool-cleansing skinheads, all filled to the gills with vodka and popping Viagra, all looking at me not so much as the only possible designated driver within five thousand miles, but more like someone on whom they can act out their nasty, retributive anti-American rage.

While pausing to consider the bill, how many rubles make a dollar, whether this is a tipping locale, I also think about inviting this willing sexpot upstairs. Strangely, I don't find that idea appealing. My disinterest also tells me that I won't be accepting the pending *dacha* outing invitation, which augurs nothing but sobriety suicide. With everything about her being so, so hot, why, I wonder, don't I have even the slightest hint of desire? But the sex I'm contemplating with her seems like an effort, a set of motions prescribed in a handbook leading to a paycheck when the shift-ending whistle blows; in short, work. I wouldn't have felt this way in a prior life under my usual influences, when I would have done it for the orgasm, the overall experience, and the satisfaction of another notch in my belt.

Without either of us saying a word, my supercilious desk clerk and I exchange the unsolicited twenty I offer for Galina's passport. I see Galina through all the bored Borises running the hotel's homeland security prostitute detection system, giving another twenty to the cabdriver who takes her away.

In the morning, my ability to wake myself up on a dime utterly fails as my eyes open twenty minutes before my noon meeting with Larisa. Dispensing with showering, I make it to the lobby just as Larisa arrives, her smooth passage through security owing, I'm guessing, to her frumpy purple down coat that's less suggestive to Muscovite security personnel.

We find a quiet corner with a chair and sofa where I help her with her coat, her body still swaddled in layers. We smile. I order tea. She's quiet, an almost seductive relief from my experiences so far.

"Who's watching Marta?" I ask, referring to her eight-year-old daughter. I know by this time that the child has ADHD, but Larisa isn't giving her drugs for fear of stifling her creativity. According to Larisa, relocating will be a boon for Marta, her ADHD symptoms, if I'm understanding Larisa correctly, becoming rebranded as just another adjustment difficulty.

"I dropped her at school," Larisa says tentatively, perhaps shy, uncertain of her English or disappointed in me. "My mother will pick her up. Was your trip okay?"

"Yes. Fine. Aeroflot was good," I say, hoping she likes me complimenting her national airline. "You know we have Bolshoi tickets tonight?"

"Of course I remember," she says. "It's across the street. They built an entire new one. Temporary. They remodel the old one. You like to see?"

Accepting, I get my first lesson about Russian cities, which is that "across the street" is more like "across town," their streets being more like mammoth squares you could run tanks down and land transports on. Crossing the first, she slips her hand around my arm, us now a bundled Russian version of the farmers in that painting *American Gothic*. We pass the Bolshoi.

"Bolshoi is Russian for big house," Larisa says.

"Where we're going tonight, right?"

"Yes," she says. "And now I go home to change for that."

"Home?"

"Yes. Traffic is bad. I live beyond the third ring," she says.

I try to absorb why she'd leave me alone the first day, then wonder if "third ring" is a veiled reference to something I missed in *The Hobbit* or, more likely, the Muscovite equivalent of saying she lives in Queens out by Kennedy Airport.

"So I go. You get to the hotel yourself?" she says, pointing across the square at my hotel that, from this distance, looks about a Latvia-size country away. "I meet you at the hotel at seven. Okay?"

Before I can ask about lunch, she walks away, presumably to find her car.

Larisa dutifully meets me at seven. She looks great in the necklace with the small diamond I'd sent from the U.S.

At the packed Bolshoi, I learn that coat-checking, like surrendering passports, isn't optional in Russia. The grandmotherly coat checkers, what my Jewish Russian relatives would call *babushkas,* log in hundreds of coats with some kind of system, one Larisa says I've subverted, accounting for my coat checker's sneer, my offense being not having the little loop in the neck of my coat to hang it with.

The performance is fantastic, the center orchestra seats in the sixth row spectacular, the coat-retrieving crowd at the end a giant amoebic mass. Everyone seeks every possible bit of leverage as we pulsate towards the *babushkas.* Larisa says the mess mainly is "because most of the people are foreigners."

With nothing suggesting that an invitation to my room would be well-received, Larisa leaves me by the hotel, meeting me again late the next morning. We trudge off to tour the Kremlin. Its "treasury"—the tsar's entire household effects intact—includes, literally, buckets of large real diamonds. Then, arm in arm, we slog our way to the Pushkin Museum for a Larisa-narrated, extremely detailed tour of Russian paintings. Then lunch at a Georgian restaurant recommended in *Fodor's*.

"How did you like the ballet?" I ask over coffee and some late-afternoon pickled fish, our snack before she retrieves her daughter for our first *family* dinner.

"I was talking with my mother about it," she says. "We agreed. In ballet, Americans clap for the athletic things."

"And?" I say, sensing more.

"And Russians clap for the overall performance, the soul of things," she says, staring at me, probably wondering if I'll let her get away with yet another foreigner insult.

Not wanting to dwell, I switch gears, asking about her child's father, who, I've learned, supplied their apartment and Larisa's car, and pays many of Marta's expenses.

"Does Marta see much of her father?"

"I don't let her."

"Why not?"

"He just takes her places. Movies. McDonald's. No talk. And he has a new girlfriend."

"That's it?" I ask, wondering how mentally damaging taking your eight-year-old to a movie could be, how much *talk* you actually can have with one, how Larisa knows there isn't any.

"I gave him some chocolates for the girlfriend. I told him I needed to meet her before Marta can stay over. This angered girlfriend. She said she would not be interviewed. She gave back the chocolates."

"In the U.S., if the father is an okay person, doing what he's supposed to, the mother can't keep him from having the child overnight."

"I think she is threatened by me. I hear she is older, and maybe not as pretty," Larisa says, cheering considerably.

We're in the car driving back from dinner at a restaurant where you order from a video screen at the table, an improvement over being served by normally scowling waitstaff. The robo-waiter also distracts Marta, who otherwise would have monopolized things, there being no apparent deficit in her ability to demand attention. Marta's now locked in a car seat, something I'd like for myself now that I see how Russians drive. Marta and I start rhyming words with her name, me kicking things off with "Marta barta sharta carta."

"Marta parta karta narta," Marta says, giggling.

"Now, now," Larisa says sternly, stopping Marta in her tracks like she's the German army.

STUCK IN THE PASSING LANE

It's been four days, and I've done everything right according to Ms. Danika's book—portraying myself correctly, comporting myself correctly, dressing and cologning correctly, bringing the correct gifts, presenting them correctly, even respecting bizarre Russian superstitions like not giving an even number of flowers and never whistling indoors. Yet, I'm not feeling anything from Larisa. Dutifully well-informed and attentive, like a highly trained docent, she shows up every morning, provides an informative commentary on the Moscow attractions *du jour* as if she studied the night before, then during dinner, which *must* occur before six after which she "never eats," she chats on impersonal topics like clothes prices. Strict as her dinner schedule, she never drinks, though I'm beginning to think that at least one of us could use a few.

After, she returns me by car to the Metropol unless, of course, we're seeing some guy called Spivakov, who directs the National Symphonic Orchestra, attending something else at the Tchaikovsky Concert Hall, or seeing another Bolshoi performance where I'm now pretty self-conscious about clapping.

Having done everything prescribed and not yet received even the slightest hint of warmth or affection, I'm beginning to feel resentful. Am I damaged goods that no amount of dressing up can make look right? On the other hand, I tell myself that there's no accounting for attraction and, in any event, Larisa, whose relationship history isn't pristine, could just be a real cold fish. The fact is that I'm not yet attracted to her. That's no small matter, though my distrust of my own feelings makes me think that our mutual lack of affection probably involves something that's my fault.

On the positive side, I've made it through Christmas, and I'm still sober, though that doesn't really count as the Russians celebrate their Christmas on January seventh, which lies ahead. I am, though, staring down the barrel at New Year's Eve, which, judging from the police cordons now barricading Moscow into zillions of little drinking pens, with three days to go, may be my Custer's Last Stand against vodka.

The Europe.net AA meeting website says there's an English-speaking meeting Monday nights at the St. Andrew Anglican Church at 8 Voznesensky Pereulok, the key word being "pereulok," meaning "small street," a euphemism, the concierge says, for places that no one can find unless someone very local helps them. I'm trudging up Tverskaya, Moscow's Broadway, past a bronze, horse-mounted monument to the founder of Moscow, a guy now dressed in a Santa Claus costume, glasnost gloss.

A church, I figure, should be easy to spot, even in a country that, until very recently, suppressed religion, steeples being the usual giveaways. I find Voznesensky Pereulok, hidden beside Moscow City Hall, more like a driveway. The *pereulok* opens into a fairly nice block lined with architecturally attractive—meaning, Larisa's taught me, Stalin-era, not Khrushchev—apartment buildings, bookended on the left by a decrepit-looking church that's dark with many of its windows boarded up. The meeting is in the basement, the descent to which is through an outdoor dark stairway, like entering a bunker.

The basement is mostly clear of rubble, the hall strung with work lamps and exposed wiring, like a mining tunnel. The meeting room is water-stained and occupied by just five people, hardly the throngs I expected this time of year.

I need to speak to find out what I'm thinking, but I wait, wanting to confirm that the Internet's correct, that the meeting is entirely in English, that it proceeds as AA meetings ordinarily do, which is with people voluntarily speaking and no one commenting on or criticizing them. This all being true, I wait a bit longer, wanting to see who these particular people are. They're mainly English and Australian. They all seem to agree about how great it is that they're not frozen drunk lying in some little *pereulok* at this particular moment.

"I'm Jed, and I'm an alcoholic," I say, their collective "Hi, Jed" response echoing off the bare walls.

"I'm from the U.S. I'm here visiting a woman I met online, and it isn't going so well," I say, all five simultaneously uncomfortably adjusting their asses in their seats.

"I don't know if I'm just not used to how Russian women act, or it's something to do with me, or with us, but there's a distance I didn't feel on the phone. Though I'm doing everything right to make her feel comfortable, I have no idea what she's thinking. She's very attentive but just doesn't say what she thinks. And this is making me want to drink. What I mean is that I have a tendency to feel ashamed, that there's something wrong with me, that I'm morally defective. For a guy who seeks relief in the approval of others, it's tough to be with someone who doesn't say what she's thinking, which I take as disapproval. My neediness just can't stand that."

Though there's no time limit in AA for how long you speak, I sense from the couple of "Thanks, Jed" responses that everyone's hoping I'm done. Many seem to be trying to be somewhere else without getting up, one guy looking at the ceiling, another at the floor, one having a magic moment behind closed eyes.

"So instead of feeling terrible for my remaining visit, even though this is kind of embarrassing for me, I decided to come here, to raise my hand and hear me say what's bothering me, which is what I've learned this is all about. Somehow saying I'm needy or insecure or an approval addict in front of fellow alcoholics makes me feel better, if only because it helps knowing I'm not the only one. It reminds me that it's more important to stay sober than dwell on shit like this. So, from New York, New York, I say thanks for listening."

"Thank you, Jed," someone says loudly, the MC's absolutely final throat slit gesture.

"Oh, one more thing," I say, cutting off the cutoff. I announce my one-year anniversary, a big thing for me, especially as it includes surviving the challenges here. They clap exuberantly like I know my AA friends back home would. There is at least a worldwide belief among AAers that the success of others is almost as important as one's own.

Larisa invites me to spend New Year's Eve at her garden apartment, where I'll meet her mother, the invitation a relief as the drunks have been raucous, bordering on rioting around the city. The hotel is decked out preparing to support a more sophisticated version of the same. On the long drive to her home, I learn that her mother survived the siege of Stalingrad, a city of a million that the Germans leveled. Larisa's mother's brother showed up four years later, having been a German POW, then, after liberation, a Russian one.

Running out of small talk, I ask her if she thinks Catherine the Great and Ivan the Terrible picked those names for themselves and, if so, whether she thinks Cathy was a bit self-impressed and Ivan too hard on himself and, in any event, whether she thinks their associates called them Ms. Great and Mr. Terrible? *No laugh.*

At a rather informal checkpoint, Larisa's paperwork is accepted in lieu of the twenty I readied. Since we're almost at her house, I take a risk.

"You know it's very hard for me to tell what you're thinking."

"About what?" she asks cautiously.

"About us."

"Us," she says, sighing curtly. "You know I have a hard time talking about such things."

"Why?"

"Why do you ask such questions? You see what I do. Is that not enough?"

"Actually, no. I'd like to know what you think."

"I've told you. I'm private. If you must know, I have trouble expressing my feelings. When I was married, sometimes I had to write letters to him."

"As long as you write the letters," I say, trying to be encouraging. "You told me your ex-husband was closed, but you were emotional."

"Emotional is different."

"Do you discuss us with your mother?"

"My mother? She is prohibited from asking anything about my personal life."

"I lived with a closed woman for twenty years," I tell her. "Someone who left me guessing what was on her mind, a game."

"I can't change automatically," Larisa says.

This, I'm thinking, should be the end, the video moment shown to non-English speakers to explain the idiom "Time to cut your losses." She's rigid, cold, and not just withholding but self-righteously so, Larisa apparently being a distant and unknowing disciple of one of my ex's self-help books, *I'm Okay, You Fuck Off.* Not even Don Quixote would entertain the thought of her ever changing; better luck waiting for the Pope's profile to appear on Match.

Yet I'm actually trying to garner some hope by interpreting her phrase "I can't change automatically." I'm thinking that someone as precise as Larisa would say "I can't change" if she meant never. But Larisa modified "change" with "automatically." Applying a principle that I learned as a lawyer, that interpretation is the effort to ascribe meaning to every single word used, "automatic" must mean something, which, here, can only be that she envisions some circumstance, possibly involving falling in love with me, under which she might start acting differently.

"Maybe you are this way because you don't want to get hurt," I say, avoiding the word *fear*, which, I've noticed, is an emotion Russians, owing probably to having been overrun by so many hordes, don't readily admit to. "I'm afraid of getting hurt too. And I could very easily get hurt trying to have a relationship with someone who doesn't respond."

She says nothing long enough for me to know that she thinks the conversation is over. Having come this far, conversationally and geographically, I'm now pissed off. But not "Stop the car, I'm done with you" pissed off. More like "Since persuasion isn't working, I'm going to rattle your cage, administer shock therapy to get what I want" pissed off.

And what do I want? I guess it's for her to really like me and say and show it. But why would I want that from someone I don't think I really care for? Someone who I'd barely tolerate a cup of coffee with back in New York? It's like I have an investment here that I need a return on. A transaction that I've put so much of myself into and laid myself out for that I can't bear it not bearing fruit, however forbidden.

"You know I met someone else the first night."

"What?" she says indignantly. "You never told me."

"You never asked."

"You were obligated," she says angrily. "You think I'm an item in a shop?"

"I'm telling you now," I say, "to show how much I care for you."

"You are treating me just like one of those mail-order brides," she spits out.

"And you're looking for any reason not to have a relationship," I say.

Instead of answering, Larisa takes the next exit, reenters the road going the other way, and returns me to sender. Dropping me at the nearest subway, she leaves me to navigate a sea of drunks, skinheads and police cordons enveloping central Moscow. I arrive at the hotel exhausted. With the aid of an ear that mumps made deaf, which I put to the outside, I fall asleep to the drumbeat of my heart rather than the screams of the revelers.

I spend my last couple of days in Moscow wandering around alone and seeing some local women I contact on the web. These meetings are quite easy to arrange owing to us for the moment being fellow Muscovites.

Though I'm convinced that it would be a huge mistake to have anything further to do with this emotionally closed woman, for some reason I accept when, the day before I leave, Larisa invites me to her house for dinner. Like a basketball team down ten points with thirty seconds to go, even though it's hopeless, I keep playing, asking Larisa on the ride she gives me from the subway to her home whether she thinks we'll stay in touch.

"I'd like," she says.

I'm surprised by her garden apartment, to which I've finally made it. It's new, modern, spacious and, by Russian standards, seemingly well-built. It's also furnished modestly and decorated in earth tones, a far cry from glitzy Moscow. Watching her move around, showing me the bedrooms, explaining what she plans to change to what where, is like following a bird comfortably safe in its own nest, a place where she cooks me crepes, serves me sausages and shows me family photos, all against the backdrop of a TV showing something no one's watching and yet no one turns off. Posing for a photo her mother takes, I feel her fall back firmly against my arm. Then she says she'll drive me to the Metropol instead of having me take the subway, much appreciated in tonight's zero degrees.

We're parked in the dark on a side street behind the Metropol, together for the last time before I leave. The time I spent getting to know Larisa, and the effort I made coming here, feels like a waste. She's a person I don't much care for, and someone who's refrained from sharing with me who she really is. Either way, the knowledge that I should just walk away is about the only thing I've gained.

"I will miss driving to the Metropol," she says.

Though somewhat enigmatic, I immediately know that this is her way of saying that she's going to miss me. Expressing that degree of interpersonal emotion is, I know, uncharacteristic of her. But is a person who takes such an itsy bitsy expression of emotion as such a big deal someone I really want to continue dealing with? And if expressing emotion is such a problem, where's the woman who practically melted on the phone the night I called to check that she and her daughter had arrived home safely from St. Petersburg?

"Just the Metropol?" I ask, knowing, though, that trying to draw her out like this is risky. I am, I guess, desperate to return home as someone who's completed a first big step, and not a quixotic fool.

"Not the hotel," she says. Then she leans over and kisses me lightly and very quickly, as if we're someplace like Saudi Arabia where the mere brushing of lips is such a forbidden act with such grave consequences that it alone has great meaning.

The next morning, before leaving for my flight, I look for a photo shop on Tverskaya. I'm thinking of buying Larisa a good digital camera. I vacillate about buying it, criticizing myself for trying to buy her love, wondering if it'll make her feel that way and why I'd care, asking myself if she'll take it as an assertion about American wealth and power and, mainly, telling myself that I shouldn't waste money on someone I just don't like. Unable to accept rejection, even from someone I don't like, I keep going, piling it on, like I did as a child when my parents kept excoriating me despite each one of my new hard-fought achievements. Trying too hard. It gets me too intimate too quickly with women I don't know, and avidly pursuing women I shouldn't. All I can think of is to take it down a notch. But other than eliminating dates that require visas, how do I distinguish modest from massive effort?

From the airport, I text Larisa to pick up a gift that I've left for her at the concierge desk at the hotel.

Home, I receive several very friendly emails from her, none of which I answer.

LIFE EXPECTANCIES

Back in the U.S., I run smack into a long-delayed *procedure* that my doctor's been demanding I undergo since I turned fifty. The thought that I'm now age-appropriate for a colonoscopy makes time seem like it's passing faster than the pre-procedure laxative is draining me.

I'm dressed and sitting with the rest of the recently scoped. They're waiting for rides home. I'm waiting for a chance to skip out and drive myself away. I stand when my gastroenterologist arrives in the waiting area. He's a bug-eyed guy owing presumably to all the peeping he does. Though he's right in front of my face, for some reason he speaks loudly.

"I think you have prostate cancer," he says, securing the undivided attention of everyone around.

"What?"

"Your prostate has a firm spot. Hard. You need to see a urologist for a biopsy."

I'm shocked, then regretful about having eaten all those fatty ribs, all that New York strip, every last bit of dripping bacon, and then embarrassed about all the people staring. Me—even when dying—self-conscious and ashamed.

Bug-eye, having completed the privacy-respecting, patient-centric, bedside manner portion of his engagement, leaves.

This diagnosis is throwing some cold water on this evening's date with Angelika, an energetic manager of a Westport luxury goods shop who seems eager to please. It's a relief to be dating within the continental U.S., and to be with someone who's seeking approval rather than passing judgment. But my mind is elsewhere, wondering whether the biopsy the urologist is doing tomorrow will be uncomfortable, painful, and what it will find.

Staring at the menu in the restaurant Angelika picked—macrobiotic, no place I'd ever go—I'm berating myself for not eating this shit all these years, the hard brown rice that would have scoured out all those carcinogens now partying up my ass.

All this dying thinking's making me want to rub my dick between Angelika's beautiful tits at any cost, including, if necessary, getting her sympathy for my *problem*.

"I'm obsessed with eating healthy," Angelika says, dabbing clinging drops of a whitish, viscous liquid, something she calls tahini, a salad dressing strongly resembling, in color and consistency, a more human fluid, from the corners of her mouth. "Ever since I watched my husband die of cancer last year, I've been obsessed with doing everything I can to fight cancer. I'm really afraid of it, petrified," she says, welling up, looking down at the sugarless, eggless, butterless, flourless, trans-fatless tart on her plate, an item that, by this process of ingredient-elimination, doesn't exist.

Is it possible that I just happen to be having dinner with a woman whose life's been ruined by, and who can think of absolutely nothing else but what I've just been told I've got? The irony prompts involuntary laughter that I'm squelching because I don't want her to think that I find her husband's death funny. This perverse confluence of events convinces me that I'm a dead man, and that my energies should now be directed at revising my living will to avoid extraordinary life-extending measures, saying my good-byes, dying well, leaving all my nonsexual affairs in order.

"I'm petrified of leprosy," I hear myself saying, not believing what I'm hearing. "When I was a little kid, I read a book about some leper colony in Hawaii. Fingers and toes and noses falling off. Scared the shit out of me. Ever since, I've been checking under my bed for lepers. I only stay at leper-free hotels. In leper-free rooms. Restaurants, gyms, pools, only certified leper-free."

I look up, expecting an empty chair. But she's still there, laughing hard, covering her face with her hand because, I think, she doesn't know whether she's hysterically offended or hysterically amused. In her confusion, that evening, she generously grants this dying man one of what he hopes are a succession of deathbed wishes.

It's my biopsy-taking day, and I'm on my knees on an examination table with my ass in the air. Frightened and uncomfortable, I'm listening to some male urologist and a female nurse bantering about who's going to get to "pull the trigger." They are, I assume, referring to the device I've been told will be used to shoot needles into my prostate, taking what the geologist in me would call "core samples." I'm angry that they have the audacity to treat sampling my prostate like some kind of arcade game, and that they'd talk like this within earshot, as if I'm a dog so it doesn't matter what I hear. They are, in essence, reenacting the disrespect shown by the gastroenterologist who publicly announced my possible cancer. Is it possible that these medical workers are what we commonly mean when we mention the orifice they routinely work in?

Over the several days that I spend waiting for the pathology report, I find myself drawn to the most flagrant floozies on Match, women whose photographs show them bending over, their breasts hanging in their loose, low-cut blouses like udders. These women generate strong sexual urges that I hope I'll still have *after* prostate surgery if I need it. That first post-operative libidinal tsunami, the one that blows a huge hole through the procedure's most feared side effect, impotence, must be wonderful. I'm imagining an award-winner that I'll film from ten different angles, my XXX homage to Leni Riefenstahl's Nazi-era recording of the 1935 Olympics, mine entitled *Triumph of Jed's Will*.

Gawking at the mammary-clogged thumbnails, my eye is caught by an All-American-looking beauty, the type I imagine who does orange juice ads, joins sororities, yachts and golfs, and mixes excellent martinis. Tall (at five foot ten in bare feet, she's got a good four inches on me), she's large-boned but, like Charlize Theron, perfectly proportioned, her photos displaying her in tight clothing accentuating her ample concaves and convexities. Down to her creamy, waspy complexion, she's exactly *not* the type of woman I'd ever be attracted to, but for some reason I am. All I want to do right now is make out with her in the elevator, under the bleachers, in the balcony; just looking at her is making me quiver.

From emails I learn she's Amita, a public relations consultant living on Manhattan's Upper East Side with her ten-year-old daughter. More specifically, she's got a three-bedroom apartment on Fifth Avenue in the eighties, where the uber rich live, Manhattan's Gold Coast.

Though all her characteristics would suggest that she'll be snooty, or at least wouldn't be interested in a short, wry-humored Jew like me, she doesn't seem stuck-up and, more importantly, for some crazy reason, possibly some inexplicable affection for Andy Sipowicz of *NYPD Blue,* she either likes short Jewish guys, or at least doesn't entirely rule out dating them.

We quickly spend time discovering nonsex-related things we both like—dim sum in Chinatown, the recently departed monologist Spaulding Gray, a Brazilian film festival where the oldies *Pixote* and *Central Station* get mutual thumbs-ups. With the Elmer's Glue of common interests and the Crazy Glue of insane sexual attraction both in place, now we can enjoy one another salaciously.

"Mr. Ringel?" a strange voice from an unidentified phone number says, interrupting Amita and I having "Blowout Specials": two hot dogs with the works and a medium drink at Papaya King on 86th and Third Avenue.

"Yes."

"It's Dr. Janus from St. Luke's-Roosevelt."

"Yes," I say, bracing for bad news from this new urologist to whom I've turned after losing confidence in the bozo I had been seeing.

"When I examined you a few days ago, I said that I could feel what your doctor noticed during the colonoscopy. But, with the confirmation I have in the pathologist's report that I just received, I can now tell you what I actually thought during the examination, which is that there's nothing of concern and there was no need for a biopsy. Your biopsy confirms this. You're completely clear."

Clear, I think. *Tom Cruise and John Travolta Scientology clear? That clear?* I'm overwhelmed.

"Thank you," I say, staring across at Amita, elated that, for a long time to come, I'll be able, if allowed, to stuff my equivalent of that mustard-smothered hot dog anywhere it fits; Dr. Janus, a urologist at a major New York City hospital saying, in well-chosen doctor-speak, essentially that the doctor who sent me for the biopsy has some boning up to do. I don't tell Amita about the answer because I haven't told her about the question, not wanting to be damaged goods to this ten-year younger woman.

Coming home to my Connecticut house from this eventful day with Amita in the city feels like I'm returning to a place, like the house I grew up in, where I no longer belong or want to be. Whether it's the twins being away in college, the allure of Amita and the city, or natural emotional erosion, in the two years since I moved out of the Ponderosa, my connection with this area where my now-defunct family spent its life feels over. So I put the house on the market and start looking for a city apartment, one near Amita, who, coincidentally, just invited me over for dinner, my first time in her (or any, for that matter) Fifth Avenue apartment.

"I adore you," Amita says, the two of us sitting together on the couch. Dinner is finished, the DVD over, and her daughter, despite her protests, in bed. Kobi lies at our feet. Though kind of brazen, I had to bring him; otherwise I'd have to decline the invitation I'm hoping for: to spend the night.

"I'm not aggressive," she whispers, which I take to be her way of giving me, the object of her adoration, the green light to have my way with her.

Sliding my hand up between her legs, slipping it under her dress, I'm already way beyond where I thought I'd be, up inside her owing to no undies, her rotating hips pressing hard against my fingers. Amita, I'm happy to see, is a devotee of doing unto others as hard and as deep as you want done unto you.

She leads me down the hall, past her daughter's bedroom, into hers, her bed tall like a throne. Amita disappears into the bathroom while I climb aboard and wait, wondering whether I should take my clothes off. Not knowing the door-locking situation, and not wanting Kobi to push open the door to her kid's room, I bring him into ours and remove my clothes.

Amita returns, naked, illuminated in the dark bedroom by the ambient glisten of city lampposts and car lights coming through her shades. Flopping on her back, she yanks me on top of her, pulling my dick in without pausing. I'm a little unnerved, what with no discussion of STDs or protection or prior sexual histories, and with her ten-year-old, though in a bedroom down the hall, possibly still within earshot of all this groaning. A sudden adjustment, her flipping her legs back, her toes touching the headboard behind her, me following inside, staying with her, now standing over and drilling down like a porn star, banishes all of my misgivings. The headboard banging against the wall, Amita's cawing like an excited crow. Her daughter, I think, now is either deeply asleep or deeply emotionally scarred. Amita reaches under me and squeezes my balls as I come, the holding back and letting go indescribable, my just reward for a passable prostate.

I read somewhere that the average man spends just three hours of his entire life having orgasms, a startlingly paltry sum given all the time spent maneuvering to have them. Now I want to spend my entire remaining allotment inside Amita. For us, the outside world has become just a locus for foreplay—elevators, museums, restaurants, cabs, the subway. We are unable to keep our hands off one another. I have the keys to her apartment, my very first set to anyone's, these delivered with introductions to her doormen who discreetly act like they don't know what's up.

We're just back from one of Amita's business trips to the UK on which I was invited along. I'm watching her lying on a chaise by my pool, the first girlfriend I've seen sit out there, and probably the last as the house is now under contract, and I'm shortly moving to an apartment in the city.

Coming into the kitchen, where I'm making us mozzarella and tomato sandwiches on baguettes, Amita smiles as she notices that I can't keep my eyes off the expensive, stringy bikini I recently bought her, coverage inversely proportional to cost and worth every penny.

"I've got something to tell you," she says, the not saying already saying well more than if she'd just come out and said it. I'm thinking she's pregnant or cheating or unhappy or unsatisfied or getting back with her ex or needing time apart or dying from an incurable disease.

"I've been wanting to tell you since we first, well, met. It's in remission, and I haven't had an outbreak in a long time, outbreaks being when it's contagious, but I have genital herpes."

I wasn't entirely kidding when I said I was afraid of leprosy. I think it's healthy to fear diseases, especially those I don't understand, including genital herpes, which I know nothing about. My sex education, which was in the late 1960s, was limited to the obese gym teacher just saying "don't."

"Is that the kind of thing you avoid with condoms?"

She nods.

"So I've been . . ."

"You can talk to my doctor. Only when there are sores, which I haven't had for years. That's when it can be contagious. And I haven't . . ."

"Okay. I'll talk to him," I say, thinking how much I would have preferred hearing that she's pregnant. How being told she's been cheating on me would have been a toss-up. How learning that she's getting back with her ex, in lieu of this, might have generated only crocodile tears.

I'm drizzling balsamic vinegar and olive oil on baguettes I doubt anyone wants, grateful for something to do, wishing she'd go back to the pool, declare a do-over, come in, start over and take the conversation another way. She sidles up beside me and takes my arm, the gesture probably an apology or a request for sympathy, or both, my gut reaction being a little flinch. I honestly don't know what to say, except that I'm glad I'm driving her home this afternoon, which doesn't seem like something she'd want to hear.

Her doctor, an absentminded old guy with a Park Avenue office, confirms what she said and, more importantly, what the CDC, NIH, Mayo Clinic and Wikipedia say on the Internet. I intellectually accept using condoms, something I haven't done since my vasectomy, and to look for sores when we fuck, me becoming sort of a cunnilingual Inspector Clouseau, though I haven't entirely worked out the flashlight part. I don't want to make so much of this that it makes our relationship less of an *us*. I am, though, nagged by the question of what to think of a person who fucks someone without telling them this, a pretty gigantic omission.

I'm sitting in B. Smith's restaurant in Sag Harbor on the north coast of what's known as Long Island's the Hamptons, my first time out here. Growing up in Long Island's tract housing section, watching the Long Island Expressway being built nearly through my backyard, I couldn't afford the wheels to get me out to this, its eastern end and, when I could, the traffic and the anticipated glitziness sent me in other directions, packing the family off for summers on less accessible islands in Long Island Sound, storeless Fishers Island or Block Island's varied, Great Britain-like terrain.

I know I'm not having such a good time when I'm enjoying my interactions with the waiter more than what's passing for conversation with the guests. They are a couple in a series of similar sets constituting Amita's friends. They tend to be later-life pairings consisting of middle-aged, childless, never married, heavily bejeweled women, each coupled with a male who's been divorced at least once, someone usually of similar vintage who has accepted being estranged from one or more of his children, something he doesn't seem to consider troublesome. Usually his conversation is entirely a torrent of blame directed at his ex-wife.

I'm here because I've surprised Amita by renting us a very nice house in Southampton for a couple of summer weeks, a place within a short walk of the ocean. But then there's the nightly hoopla, dinners in fancy places at the season's height with couples I'd rather not know.

"I saw Alec Baldwin here the other night," says Miranda, the female side of tonight's pairing, Miranda gesticulating spiritedly, smiling on and off like a blinking light, her enjoyment seemingly for show, not a true expression of feeling.

"He was sitting right there with Tina Fey. Of course I gave them space. We all do out here. They need their downtime."

Why, I think, cutting ever so slowly into my over-sauced meal, do I hate name-dropping so much? Perhaps it's because I hate bragging, name-dropping being bragging's lowest, most hollow and pathetic form, right down there with downright lying about having made a large charitable gift. What does saying you saw someone you know nothing about do for you, other than suggest that you could be the spotter on celebrity-sighting tours?

"Bill plays tennis, don't you, Bill?" Amita says, looking at Miranda's Bill, a guy on whom, unlike me, a sport jacket hangs well. As if he's just been asked to confirm a U.S. Open victory, Bill smiles demurely but doesn't answer.

"You play, right, honey?" Amita asks me. She knows I am a very good tennis player who, as evidenced by the subtle wince I hope she just saw, doesn't want to go where this is heading, which is playing at some hoity-toity Hamptons tennis club with a person of unknown ability.

"Bill plays every day at the club," Miranda says. "Take Jed," she instructs Bill, energetically continuing the abhorrent matchmaking, as if she's doing me a favor, completely ignorant of the fact that, unlike golf, a game essentially played *with oneself*, tennis is played *with someone else*, the consequence being that tennis, like sex, requires partners with commonality. Golf, as far as this non-player can tell, is more akin to masturbating: a single lonesome person proceeding stroke-by-stroke in a well-fertilized environment.

"You play?" Bill asks me, that being, I know, the refuse-at-your-own-risk invitation to play with him tomorrow. Now, my only possible outs are tripping and writhing about aggravating a torn ACL, or a sudden flare-up of shoulder bursitis.

For two tortuous hours, Bill and I play, me hitting the ball softly and right to him, trying to give him some practice like I'm his personal backboard. Starting rallies, he immediately aborts, whacking the ball anywhere his expensive, best-of-class tennis racquet decides to send it. Bill's mind and muscles, and the racquet, apparently not having reached any consensus about where the ball should go, the balls are ending up on abutting courts, sometimes on courts adjoining abutting courts, and sometimes, as one might expect from this magnificent demonstration of lack of skill, over the fence. My skills are insufficient to chase down most of these balls; Bill really needs someone more athletic, someone who combines say the leaping abilities of an Olympic high jumper with the ball-retrieving tenacity of a Labrador retriever on amphetamines.

I'm doing what has come to be my annual rite of unpacking, my hands once again paper-cut. I've moved so many times over the past couple of years that just thinking about cardboard boxes now gives me hives. This time I'm moving to The Montana, a rental on the Upper West Side, just across Central Park from Amita. The irony of this move is that just as we're becoming closer geographically, the emotional gap between us, at least on my end, feels like it's widening.

"My girlfriends think that you keeping your dog in the bedroom with us is weird," she says one night when I'm staying over. As usual, I've brought Kobi into the bedroom to keep him from surprising or frightening her daughter.

I just spent the day packing up her apartment for painters who are coming tomorrow who she completely forgot about. I feel like I'm making gestures to hide or slow the free fall that my affection for her is in. Her gratuitous and unfair comment about me and my dog, the import of which I don't even understand, and the revelation that she talks about this with her friends, isn't helping.

I'm considering whether to end this relationship that I'm no longer much enjoying. I anticipate a struggle, with me grappling with myself like Lily Tomlin does with Steve Martin from inside his body in *All of Me*. A self-deprecating diatribe brews: *You worthless creep. Throwing away yet another perfectly plausible relationship with an attractive, intelligent and generally decent woman. There goes your hair-trigger fault-finder. You've got the breakup in sight while lining up lips for the first kiss. You picky, intolerant, untrusting, thin-skinned, disingenuous bastard. You wouldn't accept a relationship with a woman even if she painted you with Frida Kahlo's passion for Diego Rivera, wrote paeans to you like Elizabeth Barrett did to Robert Browning, obsessed over you like Anaïs Nin pined for Henry Miller, sung your praises as exuberantly as the North Korean Presidential Glee Club.*

But the berating doesn't penetrate. Instead I feel nostalgic about this relationship with Amita, which, I realize, I've been involved in for over six months, the longest I've had outside my twenty-three years with my now ex. Though sad to let that go, that I lasted six months makes me seem a bit less hopeless, like someday I just might find a way to do this long term. And, I think, chuckling, *How could I stay with someone who implies to her friends that I've got some kind of sexual hang-up involving my dog?*

It's Saturday, late afternoon, and Amita and I have plans to have dinner at a Greenwich Village Italian restaurant with another set of her friends. Around 5 p.m. my phone rings.

"Hi, Dad," my youngest daughter says. Because she rarely calls, I'm especially happy to hear from her.

"Hi, honey. What's up?"

"My friends and I are coming into the city tonight. We're going to see a band at Radio City Music Hall."

"Oh," I say, beginning to think about the chaperoning, curfew and safety implications of a bunch of fifteen-year-old suburban girls going to a concert in New York City.

"Who's going?"

"My friends. We're meeting one of 'em's older sister and her friends there. They're in from college."

It's just getting better and better, I think.

"Can you meet us at Grand Central and help us get over there? Oh, and meet us after?"

I'm so excited to be asked by her for help, her mother having done all things possible to drive us apart, I can hardly keep myself from yelling "Yes!" though I know I have some logistics to deal with, so I ask for a bit more information.

"So your train comes in when?"

"Seven fifteen."

Doable without missing dinner, I think.

"And the concert ends?"

"I don't know. I'll call you."

"But approximately?"

"Dad. I don't know. It's a concert."

Though I offer to Amita to attend dinner subject to excusing myself when I get the call that the concert's over, she decides to have dinner with her friends by herself.

The next morning I give Amita a call. Then another. Then another. Though she usually picks up for me like I'm the White House calling, now she doesn't. Resisting my impulse to assume I've done something wrong, worried instead that something's happened to her, I take a cab over to her apartment building. Though I have keys and permission to go up, I ask the doorman to ring her, the request producing a very cagey look back.

"She's busy," he says, a response not auguring well.

"Amita, are you okay?" I ask when she answers my cell phone call from the street.

"I don't want to see you again," she says.

"What?"

"Leave my keys with the doorman. I'll drop yours off."

"But why? Is someone up there?" I ask, wondering why I'm even asking.

"No," she laughs. "You're scared of your kids. You'll never cross them."

"Okay," I say, this exit being far easier than explaining to myself why I've lost interest.

UNINTELLIGENT DESIGN

IN THE WEEKS SINCE AMITA and I split up, I feel adventurous. The idea that I stayed in a relationship for six months or so feels like an achievement. I know that six months isn't all that long, but you have to start somewhere. And now I can utter that bona fides-establishing line: "I just got out of a long relationship."

To celebrate, I'm letting myself do something entirely non-matchmaking. I'm starting a business that helps identify corrupt government officials, primarily from underdeveloped countries, and the money they've stolen, something I dealt with when I was a lawyer.

Actually, I'm in a London taxi heading for the home of Deepak Hasan, a short, charismatic Pakistani with piercing eyes and a machine-gun verbal delivery. Raised and educated mainly in England, including the obligatory Oxford degree, Deepak was at one time a senior official with an international corruption-fighting organization. He knows lots of good guys, honest people from third-world countries who know which government officials may be stealing in situations where theft of public funds is epidemic. The idea is to build a database identifying these officials. Large global banks, which are obligated to identify possibly stolen government funds, would use the database to find these people's accounts, freezing any funds that appear to have been embezzled and turning the matter over to reliable authorities like the U.S. Justice Department.

I arrive at my meeting with Deepak, which is in a townhouse that he rents in what, judging from the long drive from the airport, is a London suburb.

"Where's the computer?" I ask, referring to the heavy-duty system I had delivered a couple of weeks ago for him to use to work on our business.

"Over there," Deepak says, pointing to some unopened boxes. "Arif will be here in a little while. He's got some great ideas."

While we wait for Arif, a Pakistani database expert, Deepak pulls out a handful of napkins and his pencil. Making full use of his Oxford-inspired penchant for digressions, Deepak starts spouting non sequiturs that he illustrates with Jackson Pollock-like napkin doodles.

"You see, there's an entire community that can be connected via the entities we select, entities being the hub—"

"Deepak, what about the mapping?" I interrupt.

"Mapping?"

"Yes. What we agreed to do. Seeing what's available on

the web for the government entity maps. What have you done?" I ask, knowing it can't be much unless his special Pakistani powers enable him to work on a computer that's still in its box.

"Of course," Deepak says, flashing his most disarming device, a neon smile.

"Here's what I've done," I say, bringing out a pile of charts of government officials from otherwise opaque developing countries like the Philippines and Nigeria.

"I've been busy," Deepak says. "Interviewing."

"Interviewing?"

"Law firms," Deepak says, surprising me because he agreed to work full time on our joint venture. A law firm job, I know from experience, would leave no time for this.

"This is supposed to be a joint effort," I say, trying to conceal my anger.

"I've told them I have some commitments," Deepak says, flashing the smile twice this time, like it's the little device used to obliterate short-term memory in *Men in Black*.

"The worst part of this is," I say, standing, trying to get myself out of there to cool off, "you weren't forthright with me. I can't partner with someone who isn't a straight shooter when it comes to our business." With that, I find the front door and walk out, intent on disappearing for a long while to emphasize my displeasure. On the street, I'm wondering where one disappears to when one doesn't know where the fuck one is.

The Internet café I find smells from the fish-and-chips fry place next door. Paying for an hour of online time, I check emails, finding one from my friends taking care of Kobi saying his hind legs are stiffening. I've been trying to ignore this problem, which hasn't been easy since he stopped jumping into the Pathfinder, me now having to deadlift ninety pounds of squirming dog into the car. The diagnostic tools I deployed to find the cause of his diarrhea that mysteriously came and went when we moved to the city—expensive sonograms, anagrams, candy-grams—showed that all his organs were in top shape, the dog, other than his joints, a fine specimen. Though I don't want to think about it, I realize that, if his joints go while his organs remain fine, I probably will have to decide when his life ends, no bailout by terminal illness.

Nothing to do and nowhere to go, pissed and bored, it pops into my head to play around on a Russian dating site that I haven't used since I visited Larisa some eight months ago. I know this is unsafe dabbling, like me going to a bar rather than a deli for a seltzer. But I think of it as a test, one this Internet café is conducive to as the ubiquitous sound of foreigners speaking here reminds me of my Russia trip, how ill-conceived it was, my dangerous desperation, how I seduced myself into ignoring the truth.

To my surprise, I find an email in my mailbox on the Russian dating website. The email, a few months' old, is from a thirty-two-year-old engineer named Natalya, an attractive woman with down-to-the-waist typical-Russian-dating-photo-length reddish-brown hair that shimmers as if it's been hennaed. Though I'm definitely not going on another Russian escapade, with forty-five minutes of prepaid Internet time left and, frankly, being in the mood for a mischievous diversion, I send Natalya an apology for the "slight delay" and attach my Russian matchmaker-approved bio. Despite the obnoxious amount of time I've taken to answer, and the unreliability of Internet service at the Russian end, I get a quick response. She says she remembers me and that she's sure there's a good reason it's taken me so long. Her written English seems good. She's divorced with a four-year-old son, and has a good job and satisfactory housing in Volgograd, a modern city south of Moscow, but she's unhappy with the suitors she sees there and doesn't want to settle.

Something about her clear, starry blue eyes, her openness and her ease in overlooking my inexcusable delay, is eroding my wariness, transforming it into want. I'm a mere stone's throw away from this woman, I think. And I *am* working on getting better at giving women the benefit of the doubt. I get another email from her, this one saying she's read my long profile and thinks that I have a good heart, perhaps even a Russian soul as she's noticed that I've studied some Russian history and half my family is from there. She says she senses a possible connection and, apologizing for being forward, ventures the truism that two people don't really know one another until they actually meet.

I'm chastising myself for falling for what could be feigned flattery, her reflexive forgiveness and lack of suspicion being implausible, her interest too quick and avid, her effusive compliments atypical from what I know of her culture. I don't want to fall into another Larisa situation, meaning ignoring who she really is and, instead, letting my imagination run amuck.

But I don't want my life to be dictated by aversions that are based on single samples. That would have deprived me of the joys of blue and other smelly cheeses, not to mention the acquired taste of chopped liver. She may well be a beautiful, intelligent, heartfelt young woman who, unlike Larisa, trusts and expresses her feelings, someone willing to take great risks to find great love. Surely it's worth a few days and some airfare to find out.

Aware of the doubtful logic of embarking on yet another foreign escapade, especially one based solely on airbrushed photos and semi-canned dialogue, just before my Internet time runs out, I reroute my U.S. return, becoming probably the first person to fly from London to JFK via some place called Volgograd.

STUCK IN THE PASSING LANE

Having connected through Moscow, I'm on the flight to Volgograd, formerly Stalingrad, what the Internet says is one of the world's most oft-besieged cities in the one-million-plus category, most recently by the Germans, the death toll from the World War II, six-month Battle of Stalingrad being one to two million, two to four times what the U.S. lost in all of World War II, four to eight times the immediate deaths from the A-bombs we dropped on Hiroshima and Nagasaki. I'm in the aisle waiting with about twenty-five others to deplane, wondering about the donkey-pulled baggage cart I see out the window, curious why there's only one bag on it, mine. Isn't anyone else planning to stay?

I meet the luggage fellow and his very amiable donkey by a chain-link fence passing for the airport exit. A passerby translates that the old guy wants my claim ticket, which I know I wrapped my gum in and left in the seat pocket on the plane. Easy, I think, as no one else is looking for luggage, there's only one bag, and I can identify it. After another volunteer translation cycle I learn: "No ticket no bag." Stupid me. This is Russia, home of people who miss no opportunity to compel a bribe, this guy now choosing between the sawbuck I'm offering and adding my bag to his personal Tumi collection.

Outside the gate, on a crumbling asphalt path leading up to a coughing taxi, I see a woman who seems thinner, paler and taller than her photos, but nonetheless not unattractive in the light cast by the setting sun. She kisses my cheek and smiles shyly as we get into the taxi.

"We go to your hotel?" Natalya asks as we awkwardly join hands inside the cab.

The gloomy fields give way to a gloomy city along the banks of its namesake, the Volga River. Volgograd's wide main drag is lined with stiff four- and five-story buildings, a Depression-era U.S. federal building look, buildings by Stalin, urban renewal by Luftwaffe.

We are in my typically Russian suite, grand and meagerly furnished, the two of us looking through gifts I bought in London, mainly for her young son Vitaly.

"We can go to dinner later?" I ask.

"No. I need to pick up my son."

"Can we both go?" I ask.

"No," she says rather firmly. "Saturday. Yes? Day after tomorrow. I will have days off. I bring Vitaly to my parents then."

"But I thought you were taking time off?" I ask, packing up some Legos and a couple of games for her to take home to her son.

"Can't take all days off," she says. "Just one day. I am sorry. This very sudden. I have child and work, you know."

Though I've only got a day to wait, and I've got a whole new city to explore, the wait feels like a prison term. This is not so much because I'm anticipating seeing Natalya, as there's nothing much to do or see in Volgograd, which essentially leaves me sitting most of the day in a hotel room without Internet service or anything to read. Trying to make overseas calls involves running back and forth to the front desk. I run down to tell them that I need a line and pay them hard currency in varying amounts that belie the truth of their cost estimates. Then I run back up to the room to await their ring signaling an available line. Then I repeat the process over and over because the ring either never comes or, as they adamantly insist, I missed it.

"You do what?" Natalya asks when she appears in the hotel lobby around noon Saturday, a bit of blush and makeup enlivening her face.

"Not much," I say, not wanting to make her feel bad describing my boring day: the trudging up and down the stairways by the Volga embankment; the visit to the Volgograd Panorama Museum containing a wide angle view of a very narrow, uninteresting city; walking the downtown business district where the dominant business, which I can well understand, is the airline ticket office.

"I found the post office," I say, receiving a quizzical look. "Internet," I continue, that being all the explanation necessary as, until I stumbled upon the post office, I was the only person in Volgograd who didn't know that the post office is the place for a reliable, relatively high-speed Internet connection. Apparently the institution of the Internet café, a fixture throughout the third world, hasn't yet penetrated the lower Volga.

"And I found the market," I say, referring to a cavernous building housing colorful sellers of everything in the world, pickled.

"They are all thieves," she sneers.

"The vegetable market?"

"Foreigners."

"They looked Russian to me."

"From the east. Uzbeks. Cheats."

Later, over lunch, I ask, "Where do your parents live?" hoping she'll tell me more about them, perhaps offer to introduce me.

"They are not important."

"What do they do?" I ask, trying to take her tone in stride.

"Father manages factory. Mother is lawyer for company."

"Oh, I'm a lawyer. Your mother and I may have things we can discuss."

"It is too early," she says.

After dinner, we make our way to her apartment, which she's described in emails as "satisfactory." After a long taxi ride culminating in turns down several alleys, on foot we cross garbage-strewn railroad tracks and enter one of a collection of buildings that, in the U.S., from their exteriors, would be considered abandoned, perhaps drug dens, owing to the lack of entry doors or any other kind of security, broken windows, and the trashy smell outside.

Walking down a gulag-evoking hallway—garbage-strewn, paint peeling, graffitied, drippy—my imagination runs wild with awful images of what her apartment will be like. I'm shuddering inside from these thoughts as she deals with the three locks on her steel door. But her apartment is like a tiny alternate universe we've been beamed into; a little haven created by her father, one small renovated room containing all that life requires provided that one unfolds and refolds what one needs one item of furniture at a time. It feels like a luxury setup for a refugee. A miniature protective capsule.

Suddenly, I'm very sad. Sad and feeling unfairly favored with so much more. Worldly goods. Opportunities. Predictable rewards for hard work. A society whose safety net, though meager, keeps the have-nots from taking you down for their next meal. Yes, no one gave me anything. What I have I worked for, putting myself through college and law school, earning everything myself, no family support, no connections. But seeing someone with far less, someone so much more vulnerable, makes me feel like I don't deserve what I have, and that I'm selfish for not helping them by sharing it.

"I have this for you," she says, handing me something carefully wrapped—an iPod.

"Oh, you shouldn't have," I say.

Her sacrifice—diverting scarce money to buying me an iPod, plus the care she took to load it with her favorite songs, mainly from a band called Depeche Mode—squeezes the breath out of me like boa constrictor coils. I feel compelled to demonstrate profound gratitude, to show in some undeniable way how much I appreciate the import of her gesture saying that I'm okay, that I'm worth it. There's only one way I can do this I think as I wrap Natalya in my arms, careful not to trigger the lever that refolds the sofa.

"If you and Vitaly want to come to the U.S., it takes time and involves difficulties," I say.

I'm taken aback hearing myself all but invite to the U.S. someone I hardly know whose legal entry I assume will require undertakings from me that are premature to put it mildly. Like the mesmerizing lyrics in the Depeche Mode songs playing in the room, uplifting verse involving venerable themes like love and protectiveness and altruism, my profound sense of unworthiness is hypnotizing me into doing what I know I shouldn't.

"Not hard," she says, snuggling.

"Why?"

"I have green card."

"What?"

"Yes," she says, explaining via a game of twenty questions that Vitaly's father isn't Russian, but rather a U.S. geologist whom she met when he was consulting on developing nearby oil fields, and who now lives in Louisiana. Apparently, they're still legally married though the couple has been on the outs since Vitaly's birth. Hubby sends money for Vitaly even though they've seen each other only once in the past four years. And he did get Vitaly a U.S. passport and Natalya a green card, but he's so often reneged on his promises to bring them to the U.S. that she's written him off.

"Oh," is all I can say as I realize that the monumental immigration impediments to bringing Natalya and her son to the U.S. just evaporated in one little snap of this cuddly little lady's fingers. But as she nestles in closer, I find myself actually considering this prospect, one that, now that I know she has a green card and her son is a U.S. citizen, doesn't require any profession of marriage, though there should be some serious feeling for one another, something I lacked until I saw where she lives, was given an iPod, experienced the cuddling and heard this revelation.

Now, her initial lack of warmth, leaving me alone for a day, not arranging for me to meet her parents, dissembling, all seem like nothing more than nervousness, insecurity, the product of her understandable conflict between wanting to trust and love again and fearing yet another huge hurt. It's the behavior of an honest woman eager to give her heart, warped by a guy whose unfulfilled promises hurt her deeper than if he'd made none.

I tell myself to ignore the trappings here of the perfect trap for me, including the foreignness, the vulnerable waif needing protection, the minute gestures of affection that send me like blots of LSD, the generosity that obligates me. She looks small, pale, sweet and needy amidst all the folded-up furniture and the wire-covered windows. My heart is going out to her, and my sickness is fighting against me pulling it back.

To my real estate broker's giddy delight, anticipating Natalya and Vitaly's U.S. arrival, I contract to purchase a large seven-room pre-war apartment, one that's livable but needs cosmetic renovation that can be done while *we* live there.

"I found a few schools with spaces," I tell Natalya during today's phone call, referring to getting Vitaly into nursery school, a task I get right on as September is a few months away and application season is long over.

"No importance," Natalya says, a response I don't get. She's dismissing the importance of pre-K school that begins just a few months after they arrive, plus the difficulties of finding one that will be thoughtful about dealing with a child speaking only Russian, a language few here understand and that yields no English freebies, meaning no words resembling their English counterparts. According to Natalya, Vitaly supposedly has ADHD just as Larisa's daughter did. I'm beginning to think that ADHD is just Russian psychiatric code for children lacking Party discipline.

"They will take him once they meet you two, which they must do by May," I tell Natalya.

"What about the tickets?" she asks, referring to whether I'll send them tickets or just send money to buy them.

"I can get us a good deal from here," I say.

"But then you have to get me the tickets," Natalya complains. "And I will worry about getting them and about if they will take them here. Do you want me to worry?"

That, I'm thinking, is a rigged question to which the answers that immediately come to mind, such as "That's right, I want you to worry," may not translate well unless she can detect sarcasm in English. Really, I feel like Natalya's trying to find out if I'm afraid she'll disappear with my money. In her mind, I think, she's worried that I have secret suspicions that may lead to secret second thoughts, all leading to me getting cold feet akin to those her titular husband apparently got. I decide to bury my irritation, along with my secret second thoughts and suspicions and, instead, to try to put her at ease.

"If you want to buy the tickets, fine," I say, not wanting to hassle, hoping she's just nervous, that this isn't the first in a never-ending series of tests and concessions. "I'll send the money Western Union. Let me know the flight details."

Waiting for the flight at JFK's Delta terminal, I feel like I'm taking the wrong dog home from the shelter, or making a significant purchase where there are no returns, not even for store credit. I don't know what I'm doing bringing this woman and her son here, except that the "shelter" image suggests that this is more about helping someone I feel sorry for than improving my lot. Why does it seem so wrong, so self-centered to consider just my feelings, what I want? I feel like I'm forcing myself into a shotgun wedding without any behavior that even warrants one.

Something my father surprised me with recently makes me think I've been bred for this, the way kids were raised to have their organs harvested in Kazuo Ishiguro's *Never Let Me Go*. Lamenting the fact that I did not marry Amita, he asked, "Didn't you want to take care of her?"

They come around the corner, Natalya wheeling a large, belted luggage bag and looking tired and apprehensive. Vitaly, towing its junior league equivalent, is bouncing along like a Muppet. I hug Natalya with the little excitement I can muster. Her terse smirk tells me either my hug is unconvincing or, as my kids say, my face is betraying my feelings.

I set them up in the bedroom farthest from me and closest to the washing machine Natalya told me to buy. When we pass in the hall, it's like I'm in that *Seinfeld* episode about the "two face" girlfriend, with her, now my housemate, perpetually stuck in sallow, nasty-looking mode. I don't know this woman, probably never did. We could just as well be one of those couples Reverend Sun Myung Moon married by the thousands, people treated as fungible and expected to breed like cattle.

I give it one last shot, taking her and Vitaly on a driving tour of Manhattan, by boat to the Statue of Liberty and to dinner in Chinatown. I don't have a good time even for a moment; I feel like I'm doing penance without having sinned.

Trapped in my own house with nowhere for *her* to go, I decide to take a business trip to London that I deferred in anticipation of her arrival. But I don't want her to treat this as just a little break; I need to find a soft way of telling her before I leave that this isn't continuing.

"Is your job still available back in Volgograd?" I ask during dinner at Ollie's, a neighborhood Chinese place where we're speaking freely despite Vitaly's presence because the little one speaks no English.

"Why do you ask? I don't want that job," she says dismissively, still stuck in nasty face.

"Look," I say, "this is my fault. Sometimes I act too quickly. Don't think things through."

"What's wrong?" she says, acting surprised.

"This is a mistake. It isn't going to work. I'd be happy to buy you tickets home."

"Tickets," she scoffs. "I'm not going back."

"Well you have to go somewhere, and I'll help you. Vitaly can start back at his school at home in September. He won't miss anything."

"And I even was going to sleep with you tonight," Natalya says. She's so divorced from reality that she thinks this might make me change my mind.

"Okay," I say, glad to at least have been spared the awkwardness of refusing her offer. I let my "okay" hang there ambiguously. I don't want to hurt her feelings by conveying that I don't find her attractive. Yet no way should she think that this *loss* is giving me any second thoughts.

"I'm leaving tomorrow for a week in London for business," I say, which is true in that I'm giving the deal with Deepak one last try. "Please decide what you're doing by the time I get back."

When I return a week later, she's gone, her stuff cleaned out, even the small pots and pans and mincing devices she brought from home. My intuition tells me to check the call history on my landline where I find several with a Louisiana number, which is where her oil field-developing hubby resides. Apparently I've reunited these lovers, my fickle escapade yielding a silver lining in the form of a relationship game-changer for the long-separated couple. Though I bankrolled his wife and child's trip to the U.S., I start to feel sorry for this poor schmuck. Then it occurs to me that maybe this was their plan, one triggered perhaps prematurely, making me the schmuck.

Now my apartment is pleasantly empty except for Kobi stiffly padding around. Though I always seem to haul myself out of the barrel just before the flow carries me over the falls, why do I get in in the first place?

LIFE'S A BEACH

The summer upon me, I'm overtaken by gloom, what with Kobi's quality of life disappearing, Natalya still in my rearview mirror, the business I was starting now history, and the cavernous seven-room apartment I've now moved into a depressing reminder of a big wrong turn. Since my preferred environment is clear open space with good artwork on the walls, cleaning up and discarding unwanted things often cheers me up. I decide to buoy my emotions by undertaking the ultimate clutter-removal project: drafting the most ironclad living will imaginable.

Based on books and articles by medical professionals about what goes wrong with the usual lawyer-written instructions for pulling the plug, I decide to list, in precise medical terms, every single treatment I don't want, and every device that, should it be attached or implanted, I want turned off or removed.

I write up all the medical scenarios that often result in confusion or disagreement, such as when you're brought in freshly crushed from a car wreck and everyone's arguing about whether the living will lets them attach things to stabilize you to buy time to decide whether you're actually worthless enough to pull the plug on. In scientific language good enough for a *House* script, I describe exactly how I want each circumstance handled. After listening to myself at an AA meeting describe doing all this, I realize that I need to find new amusement.

So I pull what AA calls a *geographic*, decamping to the Hamptons, renting a house in Amagansett, about twenty miles beyond Southampton where Amita and I stayed. My thought is to spend lots of time with Kobi at the ocean, which is within a flat walk that'll be easy for him, and to lure my kids for visits. I also reluctantly put myself on Match again though, changing tactics, I decide to make do with those contacting me.

At first, I hear from no one. Oh, not really no one, but no one whom this superficial shit would ever go out with, it being difficult to imagine being with people whose pyramidal shapes and witchy hairdos subsume their waists, necks and hips. Then I switch my profile's zip code, which tells women where I live, from a New York City 10024 to an Amagansett 11930, so that women looking for guys with houses in the Hamptons will focus on me. Suddenly I'm awash in women, literally drowning in offers to come out and meet me, usually on weekends, all from women who "love the beach."

"Hi," says Carole as I open the gate to my little compound surrounded by a very private, five-foot high wood fence. She is a New York City beach lover who I invited to drive out for the day. Her face shows that she's close to my age, which makes me self-conscious about the impact of my aged face, which I recently had the unpleasant experience of seeing in the mirror with my reading glasses *on*. A personal shopper by trade, Carole is very nicely dressed and, having picked her for her fantastic figure, her actual body, thankfully, closely approximates her pictures, a far cry from my slightly paunchy, poorly clad one.

"Ride out okay?" I ask, taking her bag, which is suggestively heavy. "Yeah, I love it out here."

"Hungry?"

"Sure," she says, the look in her eye suggesting she's pleased with me or, more likely, my place.

A little lunch and then a walk down to the Amagansett ocean beach near my rental, and we're showering for dinner to which Carole is treating me. She chose a place in Bridgehampton where she's bought tickets to a dinner lecture by a sports sketch artist who's just released a book, which turns out to be like eating dinner while watching TV when there's nothing on.

Back at the house, she comes out of the bathroom fully clothed and kneels beside the couch where I am watching TV lying on my back. She undoes my pants and gives me an absolutely perfect, unexpected, unsolicited, no obligation blow job delivered by someone with a doctorate in penile studies or the equivalent in life experience. This magnificent performance isn't even the best part, which is her immediately retiring to a guest bedroom where she falls asleep, leaving me alone.

Carole rises the next morning to repeat the "nightcap" before breakfast, after which she gets into her car and, my unspoken gratitude firmly in hand, leaves. I'm left wondering why I'm not feeling awkward or guilty about not doing anything for her, or about us not exchanging a single thought. I decide that this just happens to be one of those magic moments when, as in the Big Bang, physics alone controls what happens. As the summer goes on, I get to reenact the creation of the cosmos several more times, different women, pretty much the same script.

Though I feel like a jerk, I also feel strangely, moronically satisfied for the moment, like I'm on R&R between tours of duty in the relationship wars, or I'm completing a stage I once went through but was too stoned and drunk to put behind me. It's also conceivable that, by finally spending time, however superficially, with women my own age, my orientation's changing a bit, the summer fulfilling the grandmotherly prophesy that nothing in life goes wasted.

Tooling around for the day, I'm heading east, away from Amagansett and East Hampton and their overpriced coffee bars and restaurants. Several miles of a stunted pine- and dune-lined highway later, I take a slight right on Old Montauk Highway. Writhing laterally with the coastline and vertically over bluffs carved from cliffs, I'm riding the edge of an ocean intermittently visible at heights, the road flattening out by a stretch of motels with names like the Briney Breezes and the Beach Plum, cryogenically frozen hostels from my 1950s youth when nirvana was a Howard Johnson's with a pool.

I reach a town called Montauk, bumper stickers pronouncing it "The End," the next landmass due east apparently being Lisbon. Montauk looks like it's been under some kind of scatterbrained intermittent development for decades. Main Street pierces a circular road about a quarter-mile in diameter. The circle is lined with stores only here and there and topped, on the north, by an eight-story stucco and wood building, now a condo. On the south side of the circle, there are stores named Chicken Seafood, Fudge and Gifts. On the protruding ends of Main Street, there are two luncheonettes, a hardware and a liquor store, real estate brokers, three gas stations, a potato-chip-oriented supermarket and miniature golf under a swinging plastic pirate.

I'm smitten. I enter Atlantic Beach Realty, the office nearest my car.

"*Whaa* can I do for you," bellows a woman introducing herself as Leslie.

"What's the story with this one?" I ask, pointing to a photograph of a gray boxy house labeled "Hither Hills Exclusive" in the window. "Sounds like a mental institution."

"That's the neighborhood," Leslie says, adding that the house is a ten-minute walk to the ocean. "A little strange, though."

Getting out on Harding Road, Leslie tells me that the house was built by a poor architect for himself, "poor" being the operative word I immediately see. It's on a tiny parcel. You reach the house via a sagging walkway to a front door that, though two floors above the foundation, due to the parcel's steep slope, is level with the road. There are two-story factory windows that must have come cheap, and the house is wrapped in warping sheets of old siding. Though on a very small footprint, the house is tall, offering, I'm guessing, a squirrel's-eye view into the canopies of the encroaching trees.

Stepping gingerly so as not to further destabilize the walkway, we enter a house that, like my world these days, doesn't have even one thing right, not one right angle, no room shaped predictably, nothing how you'd expect. The house was last inhabited by an elderly lesbian couple, Leslie explains, as we mount the staircase connecting its six floors, levels spinning off like irregular treads of circular stairs, rooms similar only in their differences.

"There may be a view here," Leslie says in the upstairs living room surrounded by banks of forty-eight-pane factory windows. The ceiling, about fifteen feet above, soars over a room about twenty-five feet square.

"I wouldn't go out there," Leslie warns as I open the sliding door to a three-story high deck. "They say it's falling off," she continues, her alert confirmed by the light I see where bolts should be holding it to the house. Craning to see through the trees, I catch a glimpse of what might just turn out to be a tree-framed ocean view.

A few offers and counteroffers later and the accountant bargaining for the dead owner and I have a deal, the only wrinkle being that he's utterly without authority, his client having died possessing a girlfriend, a house and heaps of ugly vintage furniture, but no will. Her sister, who can sign, is located in Egypt. After another eight months, and with FedEx's help, I close.

THE HEART IS A LONELY PUNTER

It's Saturday around noon and I'm crossing the Hudson River on the Tappan Zee Bridge heading to Nyack, New York, just over the bridge, for my first date since the summer ended three months ago. I'm noticing that my lighthearted summer attitude, the one that allowed me to live a version of the joke that prostitution isn't paying for sex, but rather for her leaving afterwards, has shifted my perspective a bit.

Though there are lots of couples in the cars around me, the world doesn't seem as entirely full of well-appointed, perfectly coordinated pairs, with me the outlier. Actually, there now seem to be more people like me; aging, acne-pocked, messy-haired, sarcastic, self-deprecating, ill-dressed and aimless. Being part of this group makes me feel less desperate, not so rushed, more accepting of whatever happens. The leash I have myself on even stretches enough for me to chuck the fucking toupee.

Consistent with this emotional truce, I don't know much about the person I'm meeting today, and what little I've learned places her so far from my experience that I don't know what to expect. From emails and phone conversations, I know that Meihua is forty-five and came here from mainland China twenty years ago. One of the earliest permitted Chinese students, she's now putting her U.S. doctorate in chemistry to work designing processes for a large pharmaceutical company while raising two teenagers. Despite growing up under what I'd assume was extreme censorship, she's well-versed in English literature, beginning with one of her favorites, *Jane Eyre*, the romantic who, I remember, didn't take shit from anyone, especially not lordly Mr. Rochester.

Meihua is yet another woman from outside my cultural frame of reference. But something I pick up about her—intelligence and sophistication, with childish whimsy—captivates me. Probably another bad gamble reflecting my inability to learn from experience. Nonetheless I'm taking a chance.

I feel like I'm channeling the attitude of the handyman helping me renovate my Montauk house with whom I'm spending a lot of time not getting things done. A two-hundred-seventy-pound, seventy-three-year-old jack-of-all-trades, Joe's entire life is left to chance. His current marriage is day to day, and seems to have been that way for all of its sixteen years. He works when, and to the extent that it moves him. He day-trades away the few bucks he accumulates. And he scavenges for most of his needs, from the twenty-five-foot municipal light pole he found at the dump now illuminating the driveway behind his self-built dome house, to meals made out of what's discarded at the docks after the boat hands carve off the easy fillets. A high priest in the "come what may" faith, he lives a chancy life surrounded by financial threats as if he doesn't have a care.

I'm sitting in the appointed coffee shop in Nyack when an Asian woman with small features and good posture enters wearing a sequined multicolor vest and a wool hat. Her hippie clothing surprises me. I guess I expected my first mainland Chinese date to be in a Mao jacket carrying a little red book.

"Hi, I'm Meihua," she says, shaking my hand, sitting, her voice a bit wispy nervous, her pace self-contained, composed. "Hope you haven't been waiting long."

"I just came in," I say, wanting to hear more of her perfect, accent-free English. "Did you study English in China or learn here?"

"When I was selected to take the exam to come here for my doctorate, I began studying, mainly because the exam was in English. They sent students coming here to a place called Guangzhou for six months to improve. The rest I learned here."

"In classes?"

"More like working at McDonald's. The Chinese government gave us five hundred dollars to start that we had to pay back right away. So I had to find work almost immediately."

"And you got to stay here because . . ."

"Back then the Chinese and U.S. governments had an agreement that we all had to go back, no matter what. By the time I got my degree, I was married to an American graduate student, and we'd just had a son, but it didn't matter. I was being deported."

"And?"

"Tiananmen Square. 1989. After the massacre of the demonstrators, the U.S. government stopped deporting Chinese students. That saved me."

I'm trying to contain my curiosity, not to sound like I'm doing a *60 Minutes* interview, though this woman's life is so interesting I can't stop asking questions.

"What was growing up like?" I ask lamely, following up on her telling me that she was a child of the Cultural Revolution during the late 1960s and early 1970s, a time when China was completely insane: schools closed; Mao encouraging everyone to assault one another; her family, due to some relative having owned some land before the revolution, branded "landlords," a "black family." Her parents were beaten at work, paraded as spectacles through the streets, often pulled out of the house at night to be beaten and shamed. Meihua was sent to live in a small village in the relative safety of her grandmother's house.

She remembers the ancient house fondly, its wood stove, stone walls, red-tiled roof, ornate carvings, open courtyard where she'd sit for hours reading, and the big tub where she often bathed with her grandmother. She also has vivid memories of hunger, fishing little eels out of drainage ditches to eat. "But then, four years later, I had to go back to live with my family because my grandmother died."

She faced a lot of death as a young child. One uncle hung himself rather than endure more beatings. Another was almost murdered for collaborating because, though he'd done so only under coercion, he had translated for the Japanese during World War II. Ironically, years later, the Communist government paid Meihua's family compensation for having wrongly abused him; secret files established that, while translating for the Japanese, he'd been spying for Mao.

"And your other grandparents?"

"Died during the Great Leap Forward. 1950s. Mao collectivized agriculture causing widespread famine. No food. My father's mother, I was told, was found in a field dead from starvation with grass and weeds in her mouth. She'd been starving herself so her children could have a bit more to eat."

The elementary and middle schools she should have attended were closed by the Red Guards when she was school age. When the worst of the Cultural Revolution was over, in the mid-1970s, and schools began reopening, she won admission to Shanghai's prestigious technical high school and then Beijing University, China's Harvard.

Sitting for a couple of hours, then driving around, I learn about intense platonic love, the only kind permitted in the China of her youth. Her boyfriend took twelve-hour train rides standing up, bathrooms unusable because they were packed with passengers, just to hand her his latest heartrending poetic love note.

"Want to see what's playing?" I ask, referring to an art cinema that we've passed several times, hoping she wants to extend the date. She says yes and my heart lifts. I steal little glimpses of her as we watch Noah Baumbach's *Margot at the Wedding*.

I'm slaloming home, my mind elsewhere, the car on automatic pilot. We trade Match emails about the good time we each had, then share our personal email addresses, each disclosing our full names, which I'm sure we both Google, my search coming up with her address, a rental where, aided by a Nyack florist, I send her a small, square vase of tightly bound, short-cut fragrant hibiscus. I'm hoping that her reaction to the hibiscus is far better than the angry reception I got to the tulips I sent in what now seems like a prior life.

It's Wednesday evening and, heading up to Nyack for dinner with Meihua, I'm mentally reliving our three evenings of phone conversations. I'm resolved, though all indications suggest a powerful coming together, not to jinx things or set myself up for disappointment. So I don't arrange overnight coverage for Kobi, who, incontinent and stiff, now needs walking and pills every few hours. I am grateful for this break from helplessly watching the painful disintegration of this noble animal, one I've seen catch fawns and then drop them unharmed at my feet.

I'm thinking about Meihua's relational trajectory: quickly marrying a fellow student with whom she bore children who are now fifteeen and eighteen; fending for herself and the infants in Philadelphia with an ex who didn't help out much; raising them in Austin where she moved about a dozen years ago to marry an even-tempered, good, honest, but, ultimately, not loved man; divorcing, moving here for a job, children in tow, son heading to college, daughter to high school.

"So what about you?" she asks as we begin our first meal together.

"Me?" I ask, stalling, the part of me that says things to impress people, now arguing with the non-people-pleaser. The latter, who I declare the winner and call upon to respond, is so shocked by his first-time victory that he's blanking on what to say.

"I know you were a sculptor and a lawyer, and you're now retired. You have three daughters. What else?"

"Well, during our Cultural Revolution, late 1960s and early 1970s, I was a druggie, drunken, Ivy League dropout hippie supporting myself driving cabs, sometimes stealing, living in a commune in San Francisco and joining the youth branch of the Communist Party. Came back East and put myself through—"

"No, no," she interrupts, laughing kindly despite how glib and stupid I must sound. "What shaped you?"

"Shaped? I guess I'm shaped by my parents," I hear myself say, skin dampening.

I explain how difficult my parents were, their berating that made me feel unworthy and ashamed, which in turn made me a compensating overachiever. Making this the first thing I explain about myself to someone who went through so much worse, and who I may be falling in love with, is such a stupid move that, I realize, I'm holding my breath, fearing how she'll take it.

"You are too honest, I think," she says, which I take to mean that I've supplied too much information, an irony since I so dislike it when women do that to me.

"What we endure as small children," I hear her continue, "especially fear and defenselessness, deeply affects us."

Staring into her eyes, my brain is racing, unable to calculate what it may mean to be with someone who understands childhood abuse, lack of trust, fear.

It's Saturday at 6 p.m., a few days since our dinner near her home in Nyack. It's the night I'm making her dinner at my place in the city.

My short ribs are done braising, their fruity gravy defatted, concentrated; the broccoli rabe slightly blanched and still crunchy, ready for a quick sauté in lots of garlic, salt and fresh pepper; the potatoes just mashed, milky, buttery, parmesany and a bit garlicky. The doorman buzzes that I have a visitor and, before running to the door to await her, I set out some thin-sliced Iberian ham, a saucer of Niçoise olives, some freshly cubed honeydew melon, a bottle of cold California sauvignon blanc, a wine glass for her and a tumbler of seltzer on ice for me.

Standing in my doorway watching the elevator open, I force myself to breathe as she steps out. She gives me a tiny wave and then, squeezing by me, a little kiss, our first.

She removes her shoes and hands me her coat and a CD, something by Diana Krall, who I don't know, which means nothing since the only music I know anything about is jazz.

I put the CD on in the kitchen as she stands with me by the stove asking cooking questions, me showing what's for dinner, touching her back for the first time, legs slightly brushing. Then Krall starts singing something with a chorus about "popsicle toes."

I turn to head towards the table to pour her some wine, but she, standing between me and the table, doesn't move, blocking me, us now face to face. Wrapping our arms around each other, we sway to the music, small, close movements.

We're kissing, pressing together, staring into one another's eyes. I reach behind and shut down the stove as we move slowly towards the bedroom where, laying her back on the bed, I slowly undress her, then slowly sample every flavorful part of her body, every tasty spot my hungry tongue can find, nothing overlooked, nothing refused.

The next morning, because she has to go home to take care of her daughter, reluctantly, I let her go, driving her home. When I return, after walking Kobi, I put Krall on again, hearing for the first time the verses that lovemaking left behind.

That night, in bed and lonely for someone in particular, running my hand behind my pillow, I find Meihua's black slip, scented and folded.

I want to see Meihua as much as possible. This means working around both her work schedule and the time she spends taking care of her daughter. Her rental apartment, tight temporary quarters, is too small for me to stay over; we'd be interfering with her daughter's privacy and vice versa. Weekdays I drive up to take her out to dinner. Weekends she spends a night or two with me. In between, I supervise finishing renovating my Montauk house, that beautifully minimal cube where, the more I look, the more wood I find rotting from the effects of the area's predominant feature—saltwater.

The Long Island Sound is a mile to the north, the Atlantic a quarter mile to the south, wind whipping their salts across the house, the benefits of ocean-moderated temperatures offset by corrosive salinity and high humidity. I've had workers breaking the house down, restoring salvageable parts, fabricating new ones, then carefully reassembling it like a vintage Coke machine, embellishing nothing and, to the contrary, removing elements that detract from its minimalism, replacing them with simpler solutions that ensure structural integrity.

"So how far is it?" Meihua asks as I make the best headway I can on the Long Island Expressway, my Nissan Pathfinder stuffed with a disassembled bedframe and kitchen stuff, all for the Montauk house, plus Kobi. I am seeing Meihua wearing her glasses for the first time. This is a new perspective. When she takes them off, I see a mischievous young girl.

"About another hour and a half. Do you want to stop for lunch?"

"I can wait. Can you?"

"I can't wait. But not for lunch," I say, slipping my hand into hers.

"Will this be the first time out there?" she asks.

"First home-cooked Montauk lunch?"

"No," she says, squeezing my hand.

Though Montauk in December usually is warmer than New York City, the house, which has electric heat that I mostly keep off, is stone cold when we arrive after picking up a mattress from the broker's office where I had it shipped. Electric heat, though, I discover, comes on fast, quickly warming the bedroom in which I'm having the entirely new experience of watching a woman handle what all those before her delegated to the man: furniture assembly.

Precisely, meticulously, confidently, Meihua wields the battery-operated drill like a laparoscope, quickly connecting the frame parts, attaching the headboard, anchoring the mattress slats and supports. We break the hermetically sealed plastic holding the queen-size latex mattress in its packing tube. The latex extrusion, expanding with air, jumps out just in time for me to throw her down on it and dive face-first where I've wanted to be all day, between her legs.

Meihua's skin looks naturally perfectly tanned all over, including around her vagina, where the swelling, moist scarlet inside, set against the darker skin, looks like the ripe interior of the fig Alan Bates so erotically describes eating in *Women in Love*. And now, I am, as he said, putting my mouth to the crack, sucking the sap, feeling the connectivity as I pull back, feigning stopping, then surprising her by returning, then repeating the teasing again and again. Meihua moans, clutching the mattress and then picking me up by my hair and pulling me up and inside her.

The electric heat has turned the room into an oven, which is good because otherwise we'd be cold as neither of us has the energy to find blankets. Lying naked with Meihua, face to face on our sides, lips just touching, I feel like I'm looking into a mirror of myself though without my demons. It isn't that my slate's been cleaned by contrition. And it isn't that sense of approval I falsely infer from the acceptance I read into lovemaking. It feels how I imagine I would at birth: too new to be accused of doing anything wrong, unarguably clean.

After a home-cooked dinner, the cherry hot, cast-iron stove heating the living room, we're lying together under a blanket on the sofa, her reading, me acting like I'm reading but really wondering why this is working. I'm thinking about the Asian face, smooth, rounded, almost embryonic and, in that way, naïve. Her face is unthreatening, a far cry from how Caucasian physiognomies make me feel. Then there's her courage to be vulnerable with me, despite tightly woven defenses, readily betraying the depth of her longing. And there's her concern for me, for what wounded me as a child and still makes me tick, wounds that, as she says in a birthday poem she writes for me, she hopes to help heal.

"Darling," Meihua murmurs during the ride back, surprising me with this arcane shtick term usually used by a woman dressed in an evening gown who elongates the "dah" while flicking ashes from her cigarette holder. But Meihua says it while massaging my neck, so it's no joke. "What are you doing this week?" she asks.

"Oh, nothing. Just more relaxing."

"I wish I didn't have to work."

"Relaxing is tough," I say. "You get no sympathy. No one wants to hear your complaints."

"I'd enjoy my job if I didn't have to deal with the politics," Meihua says, referring to the layers of bureaucracy above her at her company. People with no scientific training supervising scientists. Administrators who, though variously incompetent, the company seems reluctant to fire, possibly because of their age or longevity, and some perhaps because they're women.

"Deb keeps giving me assignments and then doesn't want to hear the results because she won't understand them, won't know what to do next. Then she claims in my review that I'm not a team player, not keeping her in the loop, when there is no loop, just a dead end."

"But you took some of the results to her boss, right?"

"Yeah. She told me to and then denied it, criticizing me for going over her head. Now she wants me to go with her to out-of-town conferences that are mostly wastes of time. She wants company. I just don't have the time."

"There's nothing you can do, right, except quit, and it's too early for that. How long do you get for lunch?"

"I can take whatever I want if I don't have a meeting. Why?"

"I was thinking," I say, pausing, wondering if she'll think this is kinky, and if she thinks kinky is bad. "Maybe I could meet you at your apartment during the week. You know. *Have lunch.*"

Meihua's looking straight at the windshield. I'm watching her, and I'm pretty sure I'm detecting the corners of her mouth rising, the beginnings of an upturned crescent. Leaning over, holding herself up with her hands on my upper thigh, she whispers, "Darling, that would be wonderful" in my ear, then plants firm little kisses that send bubbles up my nape, first inside my ear, then down my neck.

I'm assembling cornmeal-breaded fried green tomatoes, feta cheese and fresh basil on Dijon-slathered, sliced brioche buns, the *appetizer* for today's first of what I hope are many Nyack *lunches*. And I'm thinking about Meihua calling me "darling" all the time. Just before leaving the house, on a hunch from our first encounter—when she mentioned a couple of old English novels she liked in her teens—I find a public domain copy of *Jane Eyre* on the web. I search for "darling," the word coming up nearly twenty times, initially in reference to children and puppies, but later as how the tortured, love-struck Lord

Rochester refers to his "living darling," the tortured, love-struck proletarian maid Jane.

Researching further, I learn that an early film version starring Susannah York and George Scott was a huge hit in the late 1970s in China when Meihua was coming of age. This is when the Chinese, recovering from the Cultural Revolution, were starved for stories of passionate love. *Jane Eyre* was made censor-friendly by touting its "rebellion against social classes" theme. The film became so famous in China that the dubbers—the Mandarin voices stuffed into the English actors' mouths—became superstars. Such unusually great care was taken with the translation that the dubbing script too became famous.

I'm using my key to Meihua's building for the first time, glad there's no doorman, only an ascent of rickety stairs past a broken mailbox and a nonworking hallway light. As I'm setting out lunch, I hear her key turning. I meet her at the door, where we unanimously decide to make the sandwiches dessert.

I'm not sure exactly why I get a special thrill making love with Meihua in daylight. Perhaps everything being visible, no night's illicit cover, makes it feel purer, deeper, truer. Or maybe it's just that this is when we're supposed to be working, and it's just plain hot to fuck when you're supposed to be doing something else.

In the illuminating daylight, I unbutton and carefully fold Meihua's blouse so she can wear it back to work. Her flat belly heaves, meeting my lips as I bend to kiss it. Doing the same with her skirt and translucent black tights, I rub her feet to warm them, then suck her toes, then work my way up the inside of her thighs where I'm far less careful with her undies, wrinkles in them not noticeable to her coworkers.

But just then she throws me off, like I've hurt her or done something wrong. I'm startled, but now she's on top, straddling me, lifting up, removing my underpants, playfully reaching down, taking me inside her, then pumping, her orgasm shuddering her hips so violently for what seems like so long that my dick feels like it's breaking off.

"I've got to go back to those nut jobs," she says as we finish off the sandwiches, swiping the crumbs off the bed, me shooing her off, promising as I watch her dress that I'll make the bed. "I've got to get out of here," she sighs, looking around the room, referring, I know, to buying a house.

"What's going on with that?"

"I don't know. The broker the company gave me hasn't called back."

"I'll call him if you want. You want to see some this weekend?"

"Sure. That'd be great."

"He knows the details? Your mortgage needs? Price limit? Which towns?"

"Yeah, it's a company program that helps me with closing fees and pays part of the interest. He knows all that."

"And you don't mind him sharing your information with me?"

"No, darling. Not at all."

"Okay. Just email him that it's okay to talk to me."

"Great," she says, trussed, dressed and tucked, ready to return to the corporate wars.

It's been three long weeks of weekends traipsing through Nyack and surrounding towns looking at homes for sale with Meihua and her broker, a well-meaning guy who keeps a pencil behind his ear like he's ready to take our meal order and who never lies because he doesn't say much. It's becoming clear that, owing to Meihua being sufficiently at the low end of the area's price range, what's available either looks like the Manson cult just left, or are properties shoehorned so precariously into hillsides that they should come with lifts to hoist cars up the driveways in winter.

Pursuing this task diligently, I rework Meihua's financials, doing her expense budget and then figuring out exactly how much house she can afford. I teach her about adjustable mortgage options, something she's initially opposed to, though it quickly becomes clear that it's the only way to increase the size of the mortgage she can get. Throughout all this, she's complaining about her job, which makes me wonder why she's looking for a house in a location dictated by a job she hates, and why she's considering a loan support program from a company she may leave.

But Meihua's intent on getting back into a house, removing her furniture from storage. I presume this was the kind of home life she had back in Austin, albeit with a different man. All this is making me feel confused and, as I get deeper and deeper into advising her, responsible.

At the same time, my father, who I see every now and then, is demanding attention. I feel conflicted about this eighty-two-year-old's demands for visits and his resentful tone when I don't call as often as he'd like. I ask Meihua to come with me to visit Dad and his wife in their retirement community beside an exit about halfway down the New Jersey Turnpike. She does, and I'm immensely appreciative for the support, especially since the visit includes my father's revelation that, once in a while, he gets dizzy and just falls down, the bruise on his head being a result. His symptoms cannot be explained by any of his squadron of Medicare-paid doctors, nor the massive panoply of tests they've ordered. The twenty or so pill bottles on the kitchen counter, however, all for this otherwise healthy man, suggest that maybe he's just ingesting too many chemicals.

"So I just went to a new gerontologist," my father says. "Top guy. NYU Medical. He bills 450 dollars. Can you believe it? Medicare sent me a copy of the bill. You wanna see?"

He's leaning forward on the "his" of their "his" and "hers" matching TV-fronting Barcaloungers as he says this, his footrest conveniently retracting as he extends his legs and stands. He probably should put his feet on the ground and stand more often, preferably in a place where, as here, there are things to grab onto and there's carpeting.

"Dad, did the guy have your records?"

"What records?"

"You never saw him before, right?"

"Yes."

"So how did he know about what all your other doctors did? All your test results? All the pills you take?"

"He asked me."

"He asked an old man who takes about twenty different pills a day and who has dizziness problems to explain all his tests and pills?"

"Yeah," my father says, irritated. I guess my father's just honored to have Medicare billed on his behalf by such a distinguished guy.

"And what did you say?"

"I tried to remember the pills. Oh, and I told him what happens when I drive."

"Which is?"

"Well, sometimes when I'm driving, I see huge trees. Right in the middle of the road."

"And what did the doctor say?"

"He asked me what I did."

"And you said?"

"I told him I drive right through them." My father says this proudly, as if he's telling a story about how he acted courageously, rather than one about a driving menace whose problem lies somewhere between diminished eyesight and delusion.

"Did he talk about whether you should be driving?"

"No."

"Did he ask to get your other records, or give you any suggestions?"

"No," my father says as he walks over to a little table piled high with what I assume are Medicare statements.

"You want to see his bill?" he asks again, obviously very proud that, though tied up with a busy practice treating a celebrity row of senility-facing octogenarians, this immensely busy doctor made time to commit malpractice on my father too.

Meihua's been babysitting her boss at a conference in San Francisco for the week and I'm missing her, but not the long nightly conversations recounting every self-absorbed, paranoid, manipulative, defensive thing her boss said or did that day, and certainly not the house hunting, which has come to a point where she's bidding on houses I don't agree with.

Sometimes the house presents problems she's not assessing properly, like huge looming trees representing massive takedown costs, or a remote driveway shared with a weird guy who looks like an axe murderer. Some are too pricey. Nonetheless, she bids on them, enabled by financial engineering techniques I've taught her that qualify her for mortgages that I know, once a year passes and they adjust to their real rates, she'll need a large pay raise to afford.

I'm driving back from another visit with my father, a day spent weeding and trimming up the bushes and trees around his house. The entire time, I wondered *Why?* This is a familiar theme between us, me feeling like I have to prove I'm a good person to him, doing penance so I can be less ashamed of myself. He sat outside while I gardened. At one point, kneeling to pull some weeds, he keeled face-forward into the dirt.

Heading into the toll plaza at the George Washington Bridge, I can't shake being depressed over seeing my father keel over, though I really shouldn't give a shit about a guy who basically abandoned me from the time I turned seventeen. Never asked whether I was sick or hungry or in or out of college. Never asked how I paid rent and tuition and for food. Completely in the dark about me almost being drafted and sent to Vietnam.

I just want to go home, walk Kobi, have a few beers—which I can't—and just wallow. Hitting the West Side Highway, I dial up Meihua, hoping to get her latest stories complaining about her boss over with before I get home.

"Are you back?" I ask, knowing she's returning from San Francisco today.

"I am. And you'll never guess where I am."

"Home already?"

"Sort of."

"What do you mean?"

"Well, it's a surprise. But I'll give you a hint. I just walked Kobi, and I'm sitting on a tan sofa having tea looking at a Haitian art poster."

Knowing Meihua's waiting for me in my apartment, when all I want is to be alone, is dampening my acceleration far better than the three tickets some bastard highway patrolman gave me a couple of weeks ago, tickets auguring license-suspending points for which I'm now taking a defensive driving course. I don't want to go home, but I don't have an excuse.

"Hi," she says, stepping around her suitcase to meet me at the door. She expects, I know, an enthusiastic hug that, for the first time in our relationship, I can't give. I manage an unconvincing arm-wrap.

"What's the matter?"

I mutter something about being upset about my father and sit on the couch.

"He'll be okay," she says.

"That's consoling."

"You're being sarcastic?"

"You don't even know what's wrong with him."

"I'm saying what people say to be nice, and he'll probably be okay."

"No one knows what's wrong with him, so how can you say that?"

"You're being mean."

I'm hoping that she'll sit beside me, rub my back, say it's okay, that she understands, but I'm not holding my breath. Honestly, I'd settle just for an end to this fight, our first. Why, I wonder, can't Meihua see that there's a good reason I'm not giving her my usual intense and undivided attention? It is, after all, the first time I've had to deal with the serious illness of an aging parent. To her, I'm just insufficiently ecstatic about her unannounced drop-by. I notice that I'm no longer seeing her as the courageous little girl who rose above an incredibly poor and deeply troubled childhood. Instead, I'm seeing an intellectually gifted child whose hometown in China spoiled her with attention for the honors she brought to it.

She's opening the hall closet and putting on her coat. Making sure that I'm watching, she drops her keys to my place on the foyer table, then refuses my offer to drive her home and leaves with her luggage.

With her gone, I'm left beating myself up about what happened, how it's probably more complicated than I'm making out. This isn't simply that she reacts volatilely when someone she's written beautifully crafted, heartfelt poems to pulls away, or that she's a headstrong woman who can't stand it when her "darling" is unaccommodating. It also has something to do with me. Perhaps I mislead these women who need undue amounts of attention, offering more then I know I can sustain.

The powerful repelling forces we unleash this evening blow her clear back to Nyack, not to be seen or heard from.

MISSING IN BEIJING

I'm driving north on the West Side Highway with Kobi lying in the back. We're going to our old vet in Connecticut where Kobi's going to be put down. Though I know I've given him a good life, and that this is the best decision since he can't walk anymore, I'm obsessing about a time about a year ago when I yelled at him for pissing in the house. I'm castigating myself for yelling at him for something I now know was caused by his condition.

I think of Kobi's generosity; the staff at the pound where I found him put orphaned puppies in with him for comfort because he let them maul him to their infantile hearts' desires. His consideration for humans; he rarely entered our spaces uninvited, yet let us all into his, any time, even when he was gnawing on a big bloody bone. His frustration with enclosures, what books told me was his desire to protect me, Kobi escaping pens and houses in ways that earned him the nickname Dogdini because we often couldn't reverse engineer how he did it. His companionship in the woods. Though a laggard by nature, once in a blue moon he took off like a bandit, resurfacing by evening. People miles away would call my number from the tag on his collar, asking if I would wait a while before picking him up because their children were playing with the big wolfy beast.

I'm walking Kobi outside the vet, his last sight of earth, mine of him. I'm unable to bring him in, but my daughter, who asked to come to help, now gently guides us there.

Kobi is too big for the examination table, so I'm sitting on a blanket on the floor holding his head in my lap as various fluids slowly dull his movements, then sensations, then beating heart. I realize just past the final moment that the thought I had supposed would be helpful—that I've relieved him of his misery—isn't relieving mine at all.

I don't return home for the couple of days that I spend riding around in Connecticut trying to avoid being alone, the logistics of which are hard for a loner, especially one who, like me, enforces his loneliness, not by refusing invitations from friends, but by not having any. Desperate, I drop in on some parents I knew from raising kids there, and on the people who took care of Kobi when I traveled. Back in Montauk, for diversion, I scroll through Match women.

I find a potential dream woman, at least on paper, one living near Montauk, where I wouldn't mind spending more time. But she won't take "yes" for an answer, meaning that she schedules, cancels, reschedules and so on the same fucking dinner on and off again the same fucking day, the last straw being meeting the one place I asked not to, a fancy East Hampton restaurant. When she arrives (late, of course), she immediately runs past me to greet friends. She returns to say that they're joining us. I wish them all a good time and leave.

I'm entering Starbucks in SoHo, looking through a long line for a Chinese woman with whom I've had three short phone conversations that I've punctuated with lots of "uh-huhs," the safest thing to say to someone whose English I mostly don't get. The irony is that this, my worst-English-speaking Asian, has the most English of names, Melanie, which she uses, not in English-speaking venues like Meihua's Nyack, but in New York's Chinatown where she lives on Hester, just off Mott Street, Manhattan's Yangtze River. My attraction to her, following Meihua, may just confirm that

I've got a case of the disease that my daughters recently diagnosed: "yellow fever."

The long line I'm perusing turns out to be for the bathroom, Starbucks now apparently the world's public toilet. On the much shorter coffee line, I see an Asian woman in jeans and a T-shirt. Her height is about equal to mine, which is consistent with her profile, and she looks forty, fifteen years younger than I am. Unusual for Asian women, she's very nicely endowed.

"Melanie?"

"Jet?"

"Nice to meet you," I say, shaking her hand. "What would you like?"

"Kofee mik," she says, dashing off to hover over two seats where one occupant is checking her makeup, a prelude perhaps to leaving, Melanie's vigilance obviously having been honed wrestling with a billion people for a handful of chairs.

When I arrive with the coffee, Melanie is looking through *The New York Times*.

"What's in the news?" I ask.

"I dool lo."

"Excuse me?"

"Jus look at wha to buy."

"Oh, you're looking at the advertisements?"

"Ye."

"Okay," I say, determining to slow and simplify my speech, marveling at her angelically round, sweet face and her broad, constantly flashing smile. We chatter with minimal comprehension, neither much concerned with the very evident language gap.

"So you have two children?" I ask, limiting myself to simple, common questions while grasping for phonetic footing.

"Ye. Boy and gill. You?"

I provide my specifications: my children, my unhappy marriage, and the long relationship with Meihua that I'm recently out of, the details of which, especially that Meihua also is Asian, I carefully withhold. I don't know what she's understanding, and don't much care; her simple personality and beauty are putting the lie to the mantra, one often chanted with increasing vigor as marriages lose theirs, that communication is the foundation of a good relationship.

Heading together down Spring Street, crossing Lafayette, then down Mulberry for a few blocks, I'm following Melanie, who seems to be taking us towards Hester Street, where she lives. As we turn onto Hester, her eyes start darting like she's watching for snipers. With a sudden goodbye, she vanishes through an old tenement doorway because, I assume, she doesn't want to be seen with me in her tight-knit, inquisitive Chinese neighborhood.

A dinner date and a couple of telephone conversations later, and I'm not understanding her any better, but my interest is steadily increasing. I'm imagining a relationship akin to my Amagansett summer, except it's an infinite succession of those one-night stands, all with the same sweet, beautiful young Asian woman.

But some part of me—perhaps my conscience, or where I store and learn from experiences—is saying that someone great to look at and easy to be with just can't be my soul mate. That's because *soul mating* has a strong mental component, like tolerating one another's sarcasm, taking turns irritatingly analyzing each other, deep discussions of art, movies, friends' personalities, food and the merits of one- versus two-ply toilet paper, conflicting politics and values discussed ad nauseam until capitulation or cathartic mind-melding, and, of course, punning, none of which Melanie and I will *ever* do unless, of course, I become fluent in her Sichuan dialect of Mandarin.

But why can't I call it *soul mating* when my soul mates with Melanie's on that regular basis that, if sustained over a long term, would be the envy of all those *soul mates* who've learned the hard way that lifelong, mutually enabled orgasms aren't in their cards? Why is a relationship supposed to have more than easy attraction? Liking being together? Warmth and affection? I'm intellectually and emotionally self-sufficient. I'm capable of amusing myself and leading a full life inside my own head. I just need someone to do it around. Someone I'll grow with over the years, me old, her up, which is where Melanie comes in. This language barrier might just be the shock therapy I need. Submerging with Melanie in her grassroots Chinese community, I'll be amongst people with whom I can barely communicate, people I can't do my protective, caregiving shtick with for the simple reason that they won't understand what I'm doing and therefore won't give me the shame-relieving responses I'm doing it for.

It occurs to me that this strategy of depriving myself of the responses I seek is much like something I did when my kids were teenagers. Back then, we fought all the time. Only when I stopped responding to their provocations, which deprived them of the rewards they sought, did they stop pushing my buttons. But if this Pavlovian approach does work, will it be like chemotherapy, killing indiscriminately, throwing out things relationships need, like the desire to care for and help one another, along with my unwanted behaviors?

Melanie arrives at my apartment lightly perfumed with Chanel No. 5, wearing not-too-glossy lipstick. Her nicely evident cheekbones are ever so slightly rouged, and she's dressed in a conservatively cut top, slacks and cowboy boots.

Sitting in the kitchen, eating pork and scallion dumplings and crispy wrapped shrimp that I made earlier and just now steamed and fried, I ask how her day went, and also, because she keeps stretching and massaging her neck, whether it hurts.

"It's lothin. My bo see mae me do wery filing. He sen me to ban. I come bah an see wery angr I too lon."

"Uh-huh," I say.

"Wan to leeve job soon. Sart bises," she adds, me struggling, then getting, that she's trying to get what every self-respecting Asian wants: their own business that will form the cornerstone of their future financial empire.

She lets me squeeze by to get the whole snapper, that I've been roasting in Mediterranean spices, Sichuan chillies and hoisin sauce, out of the oven. The fish crackling, its exposed eye bulging, I put it on a mat on the table and hand her a bowl of rice and chopsticks.

"You cook mor better Chinese," she says. "You ha Chinese gifed?"

"Well, yes," I say. "But I've been cooking Chinese for a long time."

"He fome wea?"

"He?"

"Gifed?"

"Oh, she," I say, guessing from her ongoing inattention to "he" versus "she" that, in Mandarin, the third person pronoun swings both ways.

"Yes, she was from Shanghai."

Making our way through the fish, Melanie prefers the little bits and boney parts falling by the wayside, then the cheeks, then what she deftly extracts from inside the head. While concentrating on the fillet, I try to piece together her story. Her American-born-and-raised

Chinese husband, vacationing in China some twenty years ago, spied her on the street in a minor western Chinese city of around fourteen million called Chengdu. He married, impregnated and removed her to a walk-up tenement apartment in New York's Chinatown, where he kept her cloistered. She bore him a second child and, unable to speak English, she generally went out only with him. Around six years ago, when he went nuts and disappeared, Melanie learned some English and her way around the subways, and found work. Since then, she's had several relationships that she's pulled the plug on. A New Jersey businessman who criticized her too much. A wealthy amateur pilot who wanted her to move to Pennsylvania and become a Protestant. An oil executive who took her family on expensive vacations, but wanted her to move to LA. A supposedly divorced financial executive whose daughter spilled the beans, *accidentally* telling Melanie that her mommy was still daddy's wife.

The evening winding down, I lean over and kiss her. I expect a cute little rebuff, one that says that she likes me but wants to go slow. But instead, she kisses back hard and deep. In the bedroom, exhibiting the same surprisingly aggressive acceptance, she deprives me of the pleasure of undressing her, speedily taking it all off.

I learn quickly that there's little subtlety in making love with Melanie, body parts slamming and grinding, breasts buoyant and firm and, in my view, very successfully remodeled courtesy, she explains, of her last boyfriend. A little inexperienced, she readily accepts my guidance about variations, quickly establishing that, in sex, she values outcome more than authorship.

With distracting guttural grunts and clawing abounding, I turn to my secret fantasy to relieve myself. I imagine that she's an Asian prostitute who's been sent to my hotel room, the two of us doing our *business* but then falling in love.

―――――

I'm waiting at Newark Airport for Melanie's flight back from China, the end of a three-week visit during which she presumably distributed the presents we bought for her family, mainly cigarette lighters, Centrum vitamins and socks.

For the past four months I've been living in her world: helping her fourteen-year-old son get into a decent New York City high school; taking her sixteen-year-old daughter to college visits; eating in basement dives in Chinatown where meals cost three bucks; sharing home-cooked Sichuan meals called "hot pot"; hanging out with her Chinese friends, all jabbering away in Mandarin; learning to enjoy delicacies like preserved, gelatinous green egg; driving to the Chinese supermarket in Queens where produce is delivered freshly killed to the extent health regulations allow; a week together in Paris visiting the tourist sites popular with Asians like the Eiffel Tower.

"I have a surprise for you," I say, driving to East Harlem where Melanie recently moved to a two-bedroom, one-bath apartment away from prying Chinese community eyes. Though a bit crowded for my taste, a couple of months ago I accepted her invitation to move in with her there during the hiatus between the sale of my old Upper West Side apartment, the one I bought for my Russian escapade, and my new place downtown in a building being constructed that won't be ready for several months. Living with her and her kids (and relatives always passing through) has given me some of the family feeling I've missed.

"I'm studying Mandarin," I say, this being my surprise, my hope being that someday I'll understand her, or at least be the white guy whom everyone stares at when he orders in perfect Chinese.

"Who teach you?" she asks.

"I have a tutor. She's from Taiwan."

"How ol?"

"Why?"

"She wan you."

"She's married."

"I know Chinese woman," Melanie scoffs, this being our first conflict, one that, unfortunately, by her tone and body language alone, I fully understand.

It's Thanksgiving, and I'm standing on Lenox Avenue and 127th Street in Harlem with my twin daughters, Nori and Helena, waiting for Melanie and her two kids. This is the first time my kids are meeting Melanie, though my third daughter isn't here because she's taking some time off from college to hang out in Europe. Rather than cook for Thanksgiving, I've made a reservation at Sylvia's, the queen of Harlem restaurants, an obligatory watering hole on presidential campaign trails and, I think, a novel place for our Chinese-Caucasian crowd to celebrate Thanksgiving.

The six of us are crammed around a table for four where, beyond introductions, no one's talking much. In any event, the din would make hearing difficult. I flag down one of the waitresses to take our order. She says that *our* waitress is the one who gave us our menus, which isn't her. Squeezing my shoulder affectionately, she says, loud enough for all the people around to hear, that all the waitresses *here* probably look like me.

"Good going, Dad," Nori says. "Just relax, huh."

"Okay, honey," I say. "Did I tell you Melanie's opening a massage business?"

"Oh, uh, where?"

"Lew Jeesee. Maybe Connicut," Melanie says.

"New Jersey or Connecticut," I say, translating, the subject triggering none too fond memories of chauffeuring Melanie all over New Jersey and Connecticut looking at potential store locations, brokers quizzing me about the nature of the business, a subject I elide to avoid insinuations about "Asian massage."

Sylvia's food is ghastly, the most fatty, salty, sugary extreme of black cuisine, all served at room temperature, apparently having sat in chaffing dishes all morning; soggy fried chicken, dried-out turkey, greasy ribs floating in an ocean of barbecue sauce, tough collard greens, watery mashed potatoes, lumpy pumpkin pie.

"Do you understand her?" Nori asks on the subway after Sylvia's as I accompany the twins to Grand Central Station to get their train back to Connecticut.

"Sometimes. Did I tell you I'm learning Mandarin? Did you know that there are many dialects in China but they all use the same characters, so everyone—"

"You're learning Mandarin to understand her?" Nori asks.

"I like the culture and—"

"So it's like you were learning Russian for those Russian women?"

"Well maybe. But I'm—"

"Why do you move into their worlds, Dad? Does she go out to Montauk with you?"

"She doesn't like the sun. Asians generally hate the sun. In Chinatown they walk around with umbrellas on sunny—"

"What does she do for you, Dad?"

"She cooks my favorite, mapo tofu. If my arm hurts, she'll massage it forever. And she got me a Nook and—"

"That isn't—"

"And someone in Chinatown who cuts my hair for fifteen bucks . . ."

"Why don't you find someone less than twenty years younger than you? Someone smart and similar. Someone whose apartment you don't have to set up and furnish, whose chiropractor appointments you don't have to pay for, whose food shopping you don't have to do, whose kids you don't have to get Western food for and get into high school and drive all over. Someone who you understand and who gets you, and who has a real job. And if she's got to be Asian, what happened to the one working at that big company, the one with the chemistry doctorate?"

"I texted her a while ago."

"What did she say?"

"She didn't answer," I say, not adding how disappointed I was.

"Come on," I say to Melanie, stopping my car in a New Jersey parking lot for another of her driving lessons. "You have to learn."

"But I ha licens," she insists.

"Yeah. A license to kill yourself," I say, her driver's license, judging from her driving, coming from someplace similar to where she got her massage license:

a Queens basement where aspiring Asians memorize matches between the anatomical word in the massage licensing exam question and the complex word in the right answer. I don't know how she faked the road test but, for the massage-cramming fee, they certify that you've completed 500 hours of massage training, though the place doesn't have classrooms or give classes and isn't a school.

I'm feeling pressure to get her driving safely. Her mother back in Chengdu, on whom her family relies to predict the future, has just picked the specific day that's *the* most auspicious to open Melanie's New Jersey massage operation, a day barely two months away. Since the only way to get to the business in New Jersey from her home in East Harlem is by driving, we're looking at a potential disaster.

"Stop," I yell as she cuts a turn so sharply she's nose to nose with another car. "I told you to stay in your lane!"

I'm yelling, which I realize isn't such a good teaching technique, as demonstrated by her getting out of the car while, I see, it's still on and in neutral, with the parking brake off, which I point out as we switch sides.

"Sorry to yell at you," I say, feeling guilty for the unproductive outburst and scared shitless about this woman driving on city streets, the FDR Drive, the Harlem River Drive, the Cross Bronx Expressway, the George Washington Bridge, Interstate 80 and the New Jersey Turnpike.

"Ees okay. You anglee becase you wan plotet me. I tang you fol heppin me."

It's Saturday night and we just finished cleaning up from "hot pot" that Melanie prepared for some of her Sichuan friends. Melanie is snuggling against me in bed, playfully fondling me.

"I need to take a shower, honey," I say.

"Lo hai to," she says, pressing her face into what I know is a fairly ripe armpit.

"I li yol smell," she says. "Fit time. Ony you. Tuns me oln."

"I like yours too," I say, which is true, including her taste, especially after a full day when she hasn't showered, me often wondering if it's kinky to ask, as Napoleon supposedly did with Josephine, that your lover sometimes go easy with the bathing.

We're making love on a bed whose headboard and legs are telegraphing every move. Melanie's son lies on the other side of the sheetrock dividing wall, and I don't want him to hear us. We sink into the position we've developed for this circumstance, me pressing flat on top of her, face to face, nipple to nipple, hips rotating.

"Is ol aliasary," she says afterwards.

"What?"

"Aliasary. Lun yea."

"Oh. Anniversary. A year."

"Yea. Wha we doin?"

"Doing? Well, it's your birthday too. And Lunar New Year. And Valentine's Day. I'll invent something showing quadruple love."

Melanie sits up and checks her iPhone, though it didn't ring.

"Things are going great, right?" I ask.

Melanie's out of bed and leaving the room.

"Something wrong, honey?"

"You want marry Monica," she says, referring to an age-old friend of mine who's married and pregnant, who happens to be half-Taiwanese, who I've introduced Melanie to and with whom, as I have periodically over the years, I had dinner last week.

"Marry Monica?"

"Ol you Madalin teacer."

"My Mandarin teacher? You've got to be kidding."

"I no men."

"Are you asking me not to have any female friends, and to give up my tutor?"

"You man. Man cal do wah he wan," she says, getting back into bed, sinking under the covers, turning away.

We're just finishing up dim sum brunch in Chinatown, Melanie's son now off to play basketball in Chinatown's Columbus Park with his friends. Melanie and I are passing my new condo on the edge of Chinatown. We pass it all the time. But every time I invite her up, she makes an excuse not to see it.

"I lever go there," she says.

"Oh, come on. You'll love it. Big. Brand new. Lots of windows."

"I lever go," she insists.

She's upset, I'm guessing, because the condo has taken me away from living with her and the kids in East Harlem, ending some fantasy she had about me permanently moving there, though she knew about my new apartment almost from the time we started dating.

"You thought," I say, hesitating, trying to delay long enough to get calm, "that I was going to live in East Harlem. East Harlem's not my world."

What I'm really thinking is that she's not my world. That this is a foreign existence, a charming life that, like vacationing in a very exotic place, is absorbing and fantastic until one of the amenities breaks down, which is when you want the first plane out. The amenity that's broken here is that, after a year, she wants a commitment, something I don't want to give, and that I can't lie or tolerate hurting her about.

It's Saturday evening and the Knicks are playing Miami, a game I'd like to watch but can't at Melanie's because she doesn't have cable. I'm also not too interested in seeing her because, since our "anniversary," she's almost always morose.

"You comin'?" Melanie asks on the phone, our time together having created expectations about me being over on weekends.

"I'm kind of tired. I'd sort of like to watch the Knicks game here."

"You no wal me alymor. We broen up," she says, hanging up.

I'm not too broken up about the breakup, which surprises me. I expected to feel like damaged goods again. Someone who just can't find his footing in a relationship. But this one lasted almost a year and a half, double the time I spent with Meihua. With the durations of my relationships apparently doubling each time, I project that, if I have three more, the final one will last twelve years, which will bring me within range of my average life expectancy. Actually, I'm feeling a sense of accomplishment and relief, and no guilt, at least not until I start worrying about who's going to help Melanie with her massage business.

I call Monica, hoping she'll be free for lunch and help me work this through.

"Wei?" I hear on the phone, which is how Chinese say hello.

"Uh. Hi."

"Jet?"

"Melanie?" I say, realizing I've misdialed, though their phone numbers aren't similar enough to explain my mistake.

"How you?" she asks.

She doesn't sound angry, what I always think ex-girlfriends are no matter who ditched who. In fact, she sounds relieved to hear from me. I invite her to dinner at my new apartment, where, when she accepts, I make her a simple Italian pasta with onions, tomato paste, canned San Marzano tomatoes and pancetta, into which I mix freshly grated parmesan and pecorino romano, using tongs to twist the spaghetti strands onto the plate in dramatic Lydia style. After dinner, we jump each other, Melanie acting as if she'd never objected to the place.

The blue crabs are hopping in Georgica Pond in East Hampton, Melanie squealing with each tug signaling a crab clawing our trolling chicken neck. She practically jumps out of the kayak as I pull one out of the net and plop it in the basket on board.

STUCK IN THE PASSING LANE

With the kayak and gear stowed away, I turn to cooking the crabs, cleaving them in half, flipping off their top shells, cleaning off the gills, then wok stir-frying them in smoking sesame oil, glad to have remembered to pull the battery out of the smoke detector before cooking. Crabs out of the wok, I reheat the oil, quickly stir-fry chopped garlic, minced pork and fermented black beans, then add and boil off a bit of oyster sauce and dry sherry, then stir-fry slivered red and green peppers and onions, adding chicken stock that I bring to a boil, then the crabs to reheat, cornstarch to thicken, a couple of egg whites on top, the whole thing served the second the eggs lightly congeal, Cantonese-Shanghainese-Jedonese style.

Sunday, having agreed to let Melanie do some of the drive back, which is via New Jersey where we need to meet a sign painter and a plumber, I throttle back comments about her blindly changing lanes, and what I've come to see as Asian women's public act of rebellion: speeding up when everyone's slowing down, and vice versa.

We switch sides just before the Williamsburg Bridge. I'm happy to be at the controls. On the other side, on Delancey heading for the Holland Tunnel, my cell phone rings.

"Hi, Monica."

"Yeah, Thursday's great."

"See you then."

I'm through the tunnel and heading towards the New Jersey Turnpike. For once, there's little traffic. I'm cruising, but suffocating because the car feels tense, like someone sucked the air out.

"What?" I ask.

Melanie smacks and curls her lips.

"You can come to dinner with us. I've asked you many times," I say.

Melanie stares, her mind, I believe, running through all the stories she's told me about Asian women whose boyfriends or husbands, the minute they earn a few bucks, have women on the side, usually hidden in Flushing or China, a ubiquitously deceitful lot with whom I'm unfairly and, apparently, irreversibly lumped.

This, I know, is the end of us as a couple. Not so much for her as for me. Though a chronicler might cite her recurrent, deep-seated and baseless jealousy as the cause, it isn't. It's just an excuse. I know this because I could just consider it flattering. Or not tell her about people I see. Or view it as a relic of her foreign upbringing, one of many that, in their peculiarity, I find endearing, like running to seize free chairs like life depends on it, or being afraid to be seen with me, a white guy, by her former neighbors in Chinatown. It's over for me because I can't see myself with Melanie. Living with someone you really like isn't enough; they have to appear in the pictures you have of yourself.

That afternoon I help her in meetings over sign design and washer-dryer installation for her new massage parlor. But we don't address one another other than about business, not in the meetings, not during the long drive back, not afterwards.

It's been four months since breaking up with Melanie. Four months during which, though I've resisted being in touch with her, I've called from time to time to check how she's doing with the business, and taken her calls with business questions. Though we're not together, I've helped with almost everything that needs to be bought, built, hung, installed, assembled, trimmed, mulched, cleaned up, written up, negotiated and finalized in connection with her massage place, including window coverings, furniture, cabinets, light fixtures, indoor and outdoor signs, landscaping, painting, a commercial lease and all the paperwork and red tape seven New Jersey government agencies required before issuing a massage parlor permit.

The store finally opened last month, on the exact date specified by Melanie's mother, the Chengdu *feng shui*-master. The oracle's reputation for successful predictions has been burnished by the store's immediate success. Its daily customer base now is generating enough revenue to reduce my guilt over exiting.

Throughout this time, I've resisted Melanie's thinly veiled offers to massage me, which I suspected would have led to activity not covered by her permit and that she definitely can't allow on the premises. Though it would have been a well-deserved pleasure, the all but predictable massage *happy ending* would have prolonged a relationship whose unhappiness even a Chengdu oracle, one who probably has never even heard of me, knows is written in stone.

A SECOND COMING

LIFE SINCE DIVORCE has been a *Groundhog Day* of *Road to...* movies, me having more sex than Bing Crosby and Bob Hope admit to, but them seemingly having more fun. The metropolis I'm now heading for, Singapore, ironically was the site of the first *Road to...* movie, this trip being, by my rough calculation, a three-book, four-awful-movie, twenty-three-hour nightmare of flying.

Since forgoing the happy ending with Melanie, I've mainly lived in Montauk, where I've been trying to avoid dating, an effort aided by the absence of interesting women on Match within driving distance of Montauk, though I would have expected otherwise given Montauk's proximity to the Hamptons.

To occupy myself, I'm doing non-dating things. I cut trails with a volunteer crew from the local hiking association. I'm mentoring a somewhat hostile, parentless seventeen-year-old about to age-out of the New York City social service system. He hangs out with me in Montauk and has never even had his own PC. I'm catching up on American literature, post-Hemingway and Steinbeck. I've been delivering frozen dinners in bulk to my twin daughters, who, stressed out in their respective graduate programs, are becoming addicted to what's become known as *Daddy Dinners*. And I've been participating in a Montauk macrobiotic eating group, a potluck gathering where the stories about what puréed vegetable cures what if taken by suppository are far better than the mushy soba noodles and soggy brown rice.

When I feel myself breaking down from boredom and isolation, I head into the city for a few days. There, I've run through the usual Match suspects: a cute Brazilian artist who, after meeting once, suggests jerking off together over the phone; a clothing designer back from years in Paris who, fluent in French, corrects mine in an email, and then takes umbrage at my "*merci bocoo*"; a woman who silently stares for almost the entire forty-five-minute lunch; a wonderful English photographer who, at forty-five, just had twins on her own, their demands relegating her dating life to four dinner dates annually, one per change of season.

Heading for Singapore, I'm happy and not too worried, though the trek bears similarities to those to Moscow and Volgograd. This time I know the person I'm meeting—it's Meihua. While tankers and barges approach one another slowly enough to trade greetings, Meihua and I are more like emotional racing vessels, small deft crafts at risk of passing without noticing, which, it turns out, is what we almost did.

One cold Montauk night, about three months ago, having already lit the wood stove and hauled in enough wood for the evening, cooked dinner and cleaned the dishes, and finished off the last of the books the Montauk library recently ordered for me, I was completely bored. So I did something I'd never even thought about doing: for the first time in about a year I checked my old AOL account from which I'd switched to Gmail. Over ten thousand messages had accumulated. Parsing through them was unnecessary since they were obviously mostly spam, mainly offers of great wealth and potions promising penis enhancement.

But as inadvertent as it was for me to go back into this account, my eye caught something definitely non-spam: an email from Meihua, one she'd sent nine months earlier. Back then, she'd immediately and favorably responded to the text message that I'd sent her on a whim, the one that I thought she'd chosen not to answer. I immediately wrote her about the near miss. She immediately wrote back that she'd arrived in Singapore about nine months ago for a new job, my text message to her U.S. cell phone number having arrived the day before that number was shut off.

We quickly caught up on our lives, our intervening relationships, our kids, what we liked about one another that we missed. We are shocked by how closely we came to completely misunderstanding one another and, as a result, never being in touch again. The near fatal miss, and the unlikely event that hauled us back up from over the brink, was such a cinematically close call that a godless mainland Chinese and an atheistic Jewish apostate both momentarily considered the possible involvement of a higher power.

Tiptoeing around, but inexorably driven to discussing the events that constituted our breakup, I write that she quite rightly thinks highly of her own views and opinions, which sometimes makes her lack empathy for others' feelings. She writes "ouch," then describes me as an exceptionally caring person who, on occasion, is emotionally brutal to others, especially those closest to me.

A week or so later, after sharing that neither of us ever felt closer to another, a salve on old wounds, tentatively, we share our views on the details of what happened, our factual renditions being *Rashomon*-like in their differences.

She thinks that I was angry to find her there after I arrived home from visiting my ill father, perhaps because I wanted to be alone, or because she didn't ask about coming over. I believe that I wasn't angry, at least not initially, just upset and confused about my father's condition. Though I could have been less sarcastic about her effort to console me, telling me "He'll be okay" felt like she was being dismissive and just trying to turn my attention to her. I hear her gasp, and then silence. I take that to mean that I shouldn't delve further, it being a bad idea to posit that perhaps she's overly demanding, or that me being overly accommodating may have created false expectations in her.

We accept one another's perceptions and extend apologies. We agree that the bad news is that we're two headstrong, opinionated, emotionally wounded people untrusting of and easily hurt by our lovers, which, possibly, is good news too.

When I invite myself over to Singapore, Meihua is both excited and concerned about me suffering through such a painfully long flight. Because I want to see her, and she's so equally enthusiastic about seeing me, there's no question about whether I'm going. I know that gestures that include suffering, like long treks and intolerable train rides, are what Asians do, their lives lived so much closer to the brink than ours, so vulnerable to supervening forces, that enduring hardship is far greater coinage in the love realm than jewelry.

In my seat, waiting to take off, I'm surveying the flight attendants on Singapore Airlines. Each is more than equal to the airline's reviews as having notoriously beautiful, curvaceously dressed, unflappable and extraordinarily service-oriented stewardesses. Yet their beauty is evoking no more of a reaction than a great view: pictorial and, after a quick burst of feeling, unprepossessing. I'm wondering about what the Singapore Airlines employee handbook obviously directed these women to hide: their chain-smoking, cranky, irrational, bitchy-sweet and sour sides.

I'm hoping that this reflects a change in attitude, or at least that I'm giving different approaches a try. I know I've been trying to adjust my behavior recently. Mainly, I've resisted doing things *for* Meihua, though I have been out several times helping her daughter look for an apartment in the city, and I did ferry all her daughter's stuff when she moved, and I did set Meihua up with a good international phone card, and I did get her prescription sunglasses so she doesn't look, as she does in her CVS clip-ons, like Kim Il-sung, and I did mail her a copy of a recently discovered monograph, *Dirty Chinese: Everyday Slang from "What's Up?" to "F*%# Off*, which I know will make her squeal and blush. Chinese who came of age when she did are so unused to talking about the various pieces of the sexual puzzle and the ways they mesh.

I've slept the couple of hours that several Ambien induced. Waking to the landing announcements, I realize that I just dreamed of freely, pleasantly, voluntarily jumping off a tall building, enjoying the anti-gravitational slow fall all the way down, landing safely in a tiny basin, all of which I take as a good sign.

Passing through Singapore immigration, luggage in hand, customs behind me, I spot Meihua shyly but eagerly waving up at me from the pick-up area. Catching myself, an avowed atheist, hoping that the dream I just had is a good omen, I realize that I just may need some form of outside help for this, my next plunge.

EPILOGUE

Making changes in response to one of my editors, I realize that I've started thinking of him as someone who insists on knowing why things happen, especially breakups. I know that he's being *editorial* in the sense that he's representing the reader, but I can't help attributing to him personally his comment at the end of virtually every relationship: "It feels abrupt," or "A bit more buildup," or "Far too nuanced," to which I say to myself, *I have to think about this more deeply? Not again!*

Truth is, I'm the kind of person who moves through things in the fast lane, speeding along perhaps too rapidly. I can't stand accompanying people to museums because I'm done with the entire gallery while they're still ogling the first painting. I tend to skim the highly descriptive sections of books, often wondering later what happened to "Arnold," whose death, I find, is buried amidst the four pages of garden description I skipped. While I don't think I'm like that in relationships, I do think I know when they're over and, rather than linger and analyze, I head for the locker room like the buzzer's sounded the end of the game.

Whether the reader likes the results of me going back and writing more about what happened at the end of relationships and why, this process has helped me. It's enabled me to see patterns, like when I try so hard to prove to women that I'm worthwhile. That attracts women who want a tremendous amount of undivided attention, which I give at the start but often can't seem to maintain. While we all should try to avoid doing things we know are wrong, trying to be a better person than I really am isn't working for me. Maybe if I don't try so hard in the beginning, there won't be so many endings.

Speaking of endings, Meihua and I had a wonderful time during my lengthy visit with her in Singapore. We picked up exactly where we were just before our last (and because only, first) fight. Then she came to stay with me in New York for a week. I cleared my schedule, only to learn on the car ride from the airport that she'd scheduled things to do with friends to the point that we'd have maybe a day and a couple of evenings together. I felt much like when I once asked her to accompany me to a graduation party for one of my kids that was being held at an uncomfortable location: my ex's house. Without any discussion, she went ahead and scheduled a business trip to Greece for that time that I learned of only inadvertently, though I never complained. This time, my hurt made me feel a bit down emotionally the first evening. The next morning, I woke to the sound of her repacking and, without saying a word, she left.

The good news is that I just hit the one-and-a-half-year anniversary of a new relationship. This one doesn't make me feel that I need to prove my worthiness, though I'm still working on changing that part of how I act. Formerly a nurse, presently a yoga instructor, she's had some unfathomably hard knocks in life, yet she's not hardened, demanding or resentful. As part of my reprogramming program, I've even held back telling her that I love her though, honestly, I know I do.

www.ingramcontent.com/pod-product-compliance
Lightning Source LLC
Chambersburg PA
CBHW050626300426
44112CB00012B/1678